A house is a home when it shelters the body and comforts the soul.

Phillip Moffit, 1986

The DESIGN PROCESS and the ART of the Single Family Home

Richard Bertman FAIA, LEED AP

Published in Australia in 2016 by
The Images Publishing Group Pty Ltd
ABN 89 059 734 431
6 Bastow Place, Mulgrave, Victoria 3170, Australia
Tel: +61 3 9561 5544 Fax: +61 3 9561 4860
books@imagespublishing.com
www.imagespublishing.com

Copyright © The Images Publishing Group Pty Ltd 2016
The Images Publishing Group Reference Number: 976

All rights reserved. Apart from any fair dealing for the purposes of private study, research, criticism or review as permitted under the Copyright Act, no part of this publication may be reproduced, stored in a retrieval system or transmitted in any form by any means, electronic, mechanical, photocopying, recording or otherwise, without the written permission of the publisher.

National Library of Australia Cataloguing-in-Publication entry:

Creator:	Bertman, Richard, author.
Title:	The design process and the art of the single family home / Richard Bertman.
ISBN:	9781864704440 (hardback)
Subjects:	Architecture, Domestic.
	Dwellings–Design and construction.
	Architecture–North America.

Dewey Number: 728.37097

Coordinating editor: Gina Tsarouhas
Layout designer: Ryan Marshall

Printed on 140gsm GoldEast Matt Art paper by Toppan Leefung Printing (Shenzhen) Co., Ltd

IMAGES has included on its website a page for special notices in relation to this and our other publications. Please visit www.imagespublishing.com.

CONTENTS

Introduction   6

The Design Process

THE PROGRAM: Identifying The Owners' Needs and Preferences   10

THE CONTEXT FOR THE HOME: The Site, its Amenities, and Constraints   14

THE DESIGNER'S GOALS   18

THE SEARCH FOR SPACE AND FORM: Creating Architecture   20

IMPLEMENTING THE DESIGN: The Completed House   80

Additional Examples   102

House in Woods Hole   104

House in Weston   110

House in Dartmouth   114

House in Mattapoisett   120

House on Martha's Vineyard   126

House in the Berkshire Mountains   132

House in Chestnut Hill   138

House in Remington Forest   144

House in Yarmouth   148

House on Beacon Hill   154

House on Lake Erie   158

House on Plum Island   162

House on the Island of Vieques   168

Thanks and Acknowledgements   173

Photography Credits   175

Introduction

This book has grown out of an interest, first developed in graduate school, to explore the mental process involved in design. How do our minds work when we design? How do we organize and assimilate information, create and evaluate options, and make decisions?

Many years ago, in graduate school, I wondered whether it would be possible to program a computer to design. At that time, chess playing was being employed as a paradigm for determining whether a machine could compete with the human brain. Initial chess-playing programs attempted to use an algorithmic process to make decisions. A move was selected based on analyzing every conceivable outcome. But, even with high-speed computing, it quickly became evident that such an approach was illogical. It simply took too much time for the computer to run through the almost infinite number of options. The human brain doesn't work that way. It seems to function using rules of thumb developed from previous experiences to make decisions.

These rules of thumb, or 'heuristics', as they are called, were not infallible, but appeared to have the most likely chance for success, such as 'gain control of the center of the board' or 'move knights out early'. A heuristic approach became the basis for generating chess-playing programs and I wondered whether a similar approach could be used to program design. Could the design process be analyzed like a chess game? Which heuristics do architects employ? Can creative thinking be described? At the time I didn't pursue the idea. The all-encompassing effort of developing an architectural practice left little time for other interests. But, understanding the creative process has continued to intrigue me, both in my sculpture and my architecture. For years, I have thought about trying to capture and track my thinking as I work, but the proper circumstance for such an effort never seemed to present itself. Several years ago, however, I had the opportunity to pursue this interest using a vacation home I was designing as a vehicle for exploring the process.

As I designed the house, I documented my thinking by identifying the information needed to make decisions, and the steps I pursued to achieve the design. During the schematic process of conceiving space and form, I recorded each successive drawing to capture both how the house was evolving and the reasoning behind my decisions to generate its appearance. I continuously questioned myself, and tried to articulate why I was performing a particular task, and what I was thinking while performing it. Of course, the very act of stopping to analyze my thinking probably affected the process. Even so, the effort has been enlightening.

This book documents that process. It begins with a description of my clients' initial desires for their house, and the complications I encountered trying to understand their objectives. It continues with an outline of the essential information I compiled to understand their site and its environmental context. I describe my own design goals as I began the design process and, through a series of sketches, illustrate the evolution of the physical form of the house. A narrative, accompanying each sketch, describes the objectives I attempted to achieve as I designed, as well as my thoughts on the process of problem solving and creative thinking. This study has been a learning tool. Although it only shed some light on my 40-year-old inquiry into whether the design process could be programmed; still, it has helped me to clarify, organize, and better understand my own thinking, and how the final built product is an expression of that thinking. Perhaps this study can help demystify and illuminate the design process for others as well.

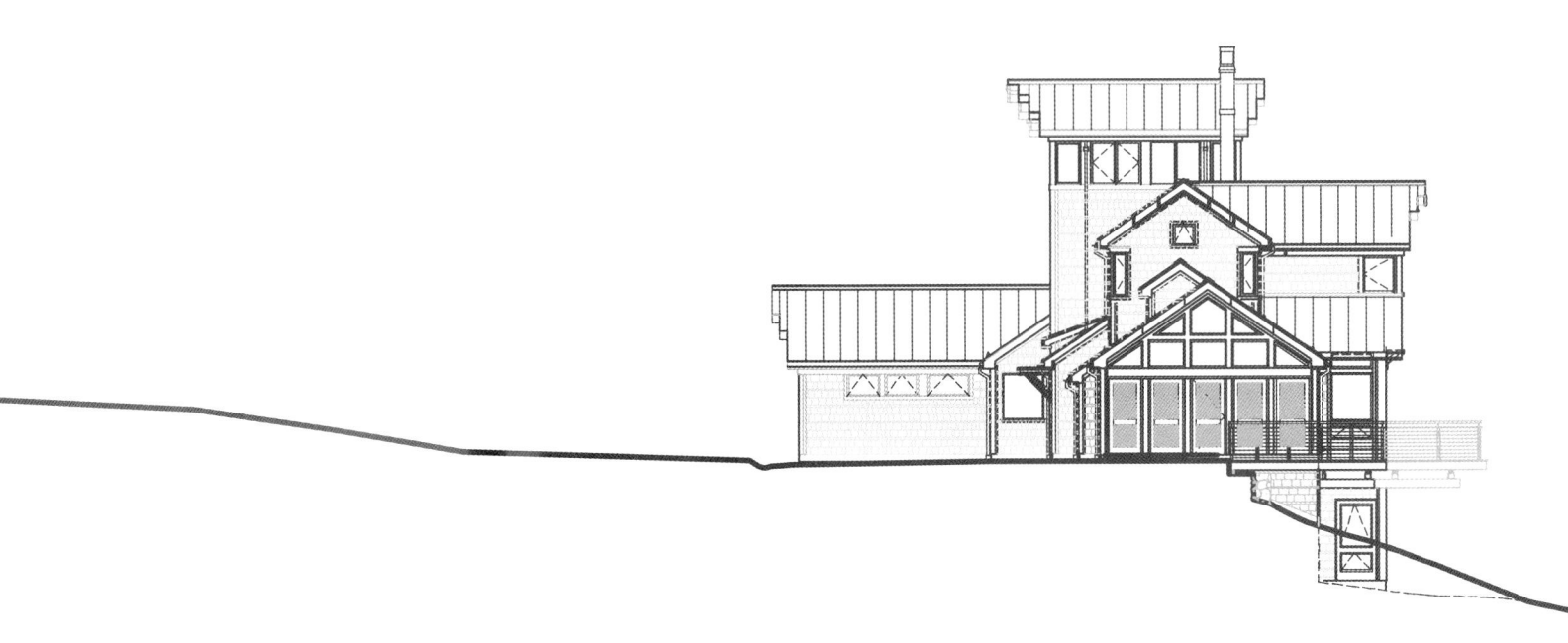

The Design Process

THE PROGRAM: Identifying the Owners' Needs and Preferences

> The formulation of a problem is often more essential than its solution.
>
> **Albert Einstein**

Design is problem solving. An inventive process, it generates graphic solutions to fulfill a series of objectives. In architecture, we call the definition of these objectives a 'program' or 'brief'. The program sets out the design parameters in detail, by establishing the requirements to be achieved for the end product.

Preparing a program involves compiling and defining a client's objectives. For a house, one presumes some common objectives, like the need for bedrooms and living space. But the designer must supplement and customize these general objectives to fit the unique intentions of their client. The process begins with a series of discussions. Usually, a client isn't precise about what they want, nor knowledgeable about what is possible within their budget. Often, they have talked with others who have built their own homes. They visit newly constructed houses and talk with builders. To jog their imagination, they may have reviewed and collected pictures of what they like. Ideally, the architect would like to be armed with a clear, well-defined program before starting design. Having a precise set of objectives simplifies the process. The more comprehensive and explicit the program, the more direct and clear the design process.

But gaining an understanding of one's clients' wishes is usually complicated. For a home, the process is muddied by its highly personal nature and a client's inexperience. Often for the first time, a client tries to comprehend, articulate and maybe agree with a partner on everything they desire. It's common that clients themselves don't clearly understand what they want. Objectives may be ill-defined or difficult to communicate. It takes a patient, concerted effort to fully elicit and grasp a person's real needs and desires.

Client objectives can be classified as quantitative or qualitative. A program will generally describe quantitative objectives that are relatively easy to define: a house does or does not have a 'master bedroom'. But it's trickier to describe qualitative objectives. The meaning of a 'gracious' stairway, 'comfortable' bath, or 'cozy' living room isn't easy to measure or communicate. Given the lack of clarity, creating acceptable solutions may require exploring many alternatives before a client's preferences can be determined and translated into a meaningful response.

As the design process proceeds, the program continues to evolve. Each client meeting becomes the setting to describe, discuss, uncover, prioritize, and redefine expectations. As the process unfolds, objectives are further clarified and priorities adjusted. For example, the initial program for this house (see following list) included a fireplace with a raised hearth. As design progressed, financial constraints dictated a smaller house. The raised hearth required more space than a flush hearth and its assertive form severely limited how the area adjacent to the fireplace could be used. The smaller sized home called for greater spatial flexibility, which became more important than the desire for a raised hearth, and led to the redesign of the fireplace.

Generally, I start the programming process by simply asking my clients to list the spaces they would like in their new home and any other considerations they deem important. I help them develop the list. For this house, my clients were a middle-aged couple from Tennessee who wished to build a second home in the mountains of western Massachusetts where they could vacation with their two grown children. The following is their list:

- a 'Berkshire cottage'
- light and sun, for example, lots of windows—as many as possible that can open
- panoramic views
- approximately 3500 square feet
- high ceilings and lots of windows in the living area with at least 9-foot ceilings in the rest of the house
- as many rooms as possible with a view over the surrounding mountains
- low maintenance/simple construction
- exposed beams where possible
- central heating and air conditioning
- alarm system
- hardwood floors—wide plank, old wood
- soundproof bedrooms and baths
- place for sound system

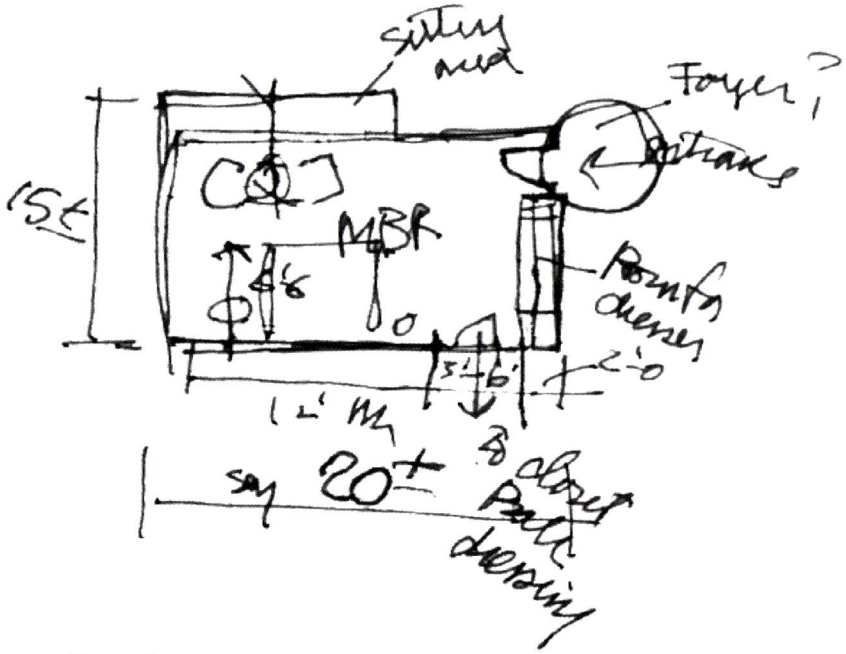

Figure 1

- master bedroom on main floor, with view, private bath—separate shower and tub, toilet and bidet in separate enclosed area, double sinks, heated floor and ceiling heat lamp
- area for desk, computer, fax, and conference calls
- three or four additional bedrooms with private baths, ceiling heat lamps
- ceiling fans
- guest powder room near living area
- open living area with dining space for up to 12 people; kitchen with granite countertops, gas stovetop, quiet dishwasher, built-in microwave, island or peninsula where stools can be used for eat-in bar
- a special 'quiet room' for reading, writing and yoga
- large stone fireplace with raised hearth
- mudroom at entrance for storing shoes, jackets, rain gear, and so on
- laundry area for washer and dryer
- three-sided, large, screened porch with view that doesn't block other views
- deck or patio with view
- two-car garage combined with new house or reusing existing garage building
- window seat

Working from these preferences, I made a list of spaces. From previous experience and through discussions with the clients, I established rough dimensions for each space by considering the area needed for likely activities, the maximum and usual number of participants, and the usual amount of associated furniture, fixtures and equipment. For each space, I developed an approximate size, sketching a diagram like the one shown above for the master bedroom. The process helped quantify the size of spaces, the overall size of the house, and some functional issues to consider as I began the design process:

- master bedroom: 20 x 15 = 300 square feet (diagram shown above)
- master bath: 13 x 15 = 195 square feet
- master closet: 8 x 14 = 112 square feet
- four bedrooms: 14 x 15 = 210 square feet; 4 x 210 square feet = 840 square feet in total
- four closets: 2 x 6 = 12 square feet; 4 x 12 square feet = 48 square feet in total
- four baths: 6 x 10 = 60 square feet; 4 x 60 = 240 square feet in total
- porch: 21 x 21 = 441 x 0.5 = 220 square feet (for calculating area, non-heated spaces are computed at 0.5 in estimating construction cost)
- laundry: 7 x 10 = 70 square feet
- mudroom: 8 x 8 = 64 square feet
- powder room: 6 x 6 = 36 square feet
- quiet room/yoga: 12 x 12 = 144 square feet
- computer area/office: 8 x 10 = 80 square feet
- living room: 22 x 20 = 440 square feet

- dining area: 22 x 12 = 264 square feet
- kitchen: 22 x 12 = 264 square feet
- pantry: 8 x 8 = 64 square feet

These areas totaled 3381 square feet. Then I added space to account for undefined circulation areas such as halls, foyers, stairs and vestibules (which normally require adding 20-30 percent more space). I added 20 percent, assuming an efficient organizational layout for the house. An efficient plan would be necessary, since the space my clients desired was turning out to be larger than the 3500 square feet they had initially anticipated. It now totaled 4057 square feet.

We discussed the disparity between my assumptions and their initial size estimate. Budget always influences design. The responsible designer walks a fine line between maximizing project potential and meeting cost constraints. At this early stage of design, it was especially difficult to estimate costs; concepts were unresolved and ideas fluid. But the disparity in size made it imperative to create an efficient layout that consumed only the necessary amount of space. A more accurate cost projection for the house would require waiting until I had developed a more evolved schematic design.

Ongoing meetings with my clients helped me better understand how their budget related to their priorities regarding: the size of spaces; their preferences regarding views, privacy, acoustics, materials; degrees of formality; connections between spaces; relationship of house to site; energy and maintenance; and quality. To further absorb their preferences, we reviewed pictures from books, magazines and the design of other houses. If possible, I will visit my clients' homes to better understand how they live. Such visits help clarify their intentions. What are their current space needs? How much do they socialize or entertain? Do they live formally or informally? Are spaces in their home decorated or utilitarian, elaborate or simple? If they have children or grandchildren, what are their needs? Do they have pets? Is there furniture or furnishings that will be retained and reused in the new home? Are there any special needs requiring specific facilities?

Over time, my understanding of my clients' preferences deepens as I get to know them, and as we explore sketch ideas that help them recall and envision objectives they didn't express initially. Knowing the desires of my clients is more than just defining the parameters for their home. I strive to comprehend their wishes and not to give back a design that's expected, but to understand them well enough to expand their expectations. If I can truly grasp their needs, then, together, we can create a more livable and enjoyable home than either of us had first imagined.

It's a dynamic process that achieves the best results through mutual give and take. I try to encourage my clients to consider ideas that may be unfamiliar to them. I hope they'll push me to justify those ideas in terms that suit their lifestyles. It is this relationship that leads to innovative but comfortable, affordable and, most importantly, livable long-term design solutions.

THE CONTEXT FOR THE HOME: The Site, its Amenities, and Constraints

> Just because it isn't done, doesn't mean it can't be done. Just because it can be done, doesn't mean it should be.
>
> **Barry Glasford**

A well-designed home not only 'fits' its occupants, but also captures and expresses the special nature of its site and surroundings. Every site is defined by a unique series of variables. Some become amenities, which can reinforce and enrich the design. Others constrain and limit solutions. Zoning codes and ordinances, site boundaries, climatic conditions, soil bearing capacity, and construction budgets are examples of such constraints. These restrict the available design solutions because of the considerable effort to change or modify them. Although I try to avoid solutions that conflict with constraints, I initially proceed as if there were no restrictions. Doing so enables me to identify limitations that may compromise design. I then try to find ways to overcome these restrictions. There should always be a thoughtful effort to create beyond the bounds of conventional limitations. Attempts to overcome restrictions often lead to more inspired solutions. It may also be worth attempting to modify constraints—pursuing a variance, for example—when success in that effort can improve results substantially.

The following list identifies the information I usually attempt to gather to better understand the context for the house and the conditions that will influence decisions during design.

Site Boundaries (Property Lines)
These establish the location of the plot and legally define its limits.

Abutting and Surrounding Properties

Are there any existing or potential, natural or humanmade features on surrounding properties, which may impact views or affect privacy or security? Are there locations on site that should be avoided because of their detrimental impact on, or from, neighbors? What is the character of adjacent properties—scale, style, materials? Should the design respond to that character?

Easements and Rights of Way

Are there any? Will they affect the location of the house by impacting privacy, access, security or views? How can the house be sited to best accommodate them?

Direction of Sun

Where should the house be sited to maximize the benefits of the sun and minimize unwanted heat gain? Are there spaces within the house that would benefit from a particular orientation, for example, breakfast areas on the east for morning sunlight or living spaces on the south?

Views

In what direction are pleasant views, long vistas and other features? Are there views that should be screened? How do views correspond to sun orientation? Wind? Are there unique vistas approaching the site, or within the site, which will affect where the house is situated? The desire to optimize views from every part of a house is typically an important objective.

Topography

A grading plan drawn at a minimum of 2-foot elevation increments provided by a civil engineer is helpful in ensuring the proper relationship of inside-to-outside space. Information from the grading plan is useful in: setting floor grades and outdoor living areas, establishing the need for cut or fill, determining proper drainage, ensuring that grades are appropriate for access and movement of vehicles, ascertaining the need for retaining walls, ensuring the retention of trees, and for the proper design of septic systems and utility lines.

Access Ways

Where does the site abut roads and walkways? How will one be able to access the property—by car, by foot? Are there natural or existing roads or pathways through the site that should be retained? Will access ways limit the location of the house?

Direction and Intensity of the Wind

Storm winds? Prevailing winds? How intense are prevailing winds relative to their impact on outdoor living? Is special protection needed for hurricanes or tornados?

Trees and Vegetation

Where are trees located? What size? What type? Are there special trees or vegetation that give a unique character to the site? Will trees need to be removed? It is helpful to have large caliper trees located on the engineered survey.

Special Features

Rock outcroppings, waterways, special landforms, historical features, geological formations or existing structures may give a site special character. Although possibly constraining, special features may reinforce the qualities of a design and even suggest a design direction.

Utilities

The availability and location of utilities such as water, a sewer, electricity, gas, telephones, and cable TV need to be identified. Will special facilities, such as a septic system or a well, need to be designed? Do they exist? If not, where can they be located? Are there setback requirements from these utilities? How will their location affect the design and placement of the house?

Water Table

At what elevation is ground water? Will ground water affect the lowest slab elevation, height of the house, septic system or finish grades?

Seismic Constraints and the Geological Makeup and Structural Capacity of Soils

Are there unique soil conditions, such as ledge or peat, which may affect the house's foundations or where it is sited? Early input from a structural engineer to establish any constraints is helpful. Test pits and borings may be needed.

Zoning Codes, Special Agreements, Building Codes and Historic Districts

What are the official zoning and building codes? Are there other special restrictions on design that must be accommodated? In addition to zoning and building codes, there may be private design review stipulations or historic district restrictions that can limit all aspects of design from the location of the house on the site, to its height, its materials, even the size of openings and the height of ceilings. Some restrictions relate to public health and safety, but others may affect aesthetic expression.

Water Features

Proximity to water features such as the ocean, lakes, ponds, streams, rivers and wetlands are major amenities, but usually have specific setback limitations and, sometimes (for example, in flood plains), minimum habitable floor elevations that need to be taken into account when setting the house.

Environmental Issues

There are times when previous site uses may have had adverse environmental effects. It is wise to ensure that no contaminants exist on the site.

The setting for a house and its relationship to the land is so important that collaboration with an experienced landscape architect is not only beneficial, but also critical. It is helpful to have that collaboration begin early. For me, it is during schematic design, after I have some understanding of the intentions of the house and its relationship to the site, so I can guide and appreciate the landscape architect's input. Often, there is a synergy that occurs between us that improves both the landscape and building design.

To gather the above information, I try to visit the site several times and walk the land in different seasons and varying times of day to properly familiarize myself with its subtleties. Once I have a preliminary design, I revisit the site to test original impressions. Also, just before construction, it is helpful to 'stake-out' the proposed scheme, to lay out the location of the house's walls. This is an opportunity to virtually 'walk' through the house, to imagine the spaces and their relationship to their surroundings, and to carry out one final check with my clients on the validity of our decisions. Often, there is final tweaking that ensures a better result.

THE DESIGNER'S GOALS

> When I am working on a problem, I never think about beauty. I think only about how to solve the problem. But when I have finished, if the solution is not beautiful, I know it is wrong.
>
> R. Buckminster Fuller

Although client objectives and site conditions are the important controlling factors in design, it is the designer, of course, who generates and develops solutions to these parameters. Therefore, the designer's own objectives contribute substantially to the direction of a design solution. For the design of this house, my hope (and the focus of my enjoyment in designing houses) is to design a special place that responds to my client's particular needs and the site's distinctive location, expressed in a fresh, non-imitational way.

Good architecture requires accommodating many factors but, to me, there are four major considerations:

1. Function

A house is a container defined by the activities that take place within and around it. Whether expressed in the program explicitly, or implied by the building type, there are a myriad of activities that need to function properly. Space must be created to accommodate these activities. The shape of spaces, their proportions, the degree of transparency, climatic controls, the relationship to other spaces and to the larger environment, as well as their visual, aural and tactile expression, all emerge from this symbiosis with the functions these spaces accommodate. Proper functioning is the facilitator of space and form, and the prime responsibility of good architecture.

2. Integration of Inside and Out

Good buildings must be designed not only from within, but their form, scale, materials, details, and equipment must also be responsive to external conditions. All the impacts of a site's physical and environmental features need to be considered in the design of good architecture. All affect a building's performance and longevity. When conflicts between internal programmatic needs and external influences occur, creative design must find mediating solutions that resolve these differences.

3. Harmony and Delight

A good building should be visually pleasing in its form, spatial expression, scale, materials and details. Aesthetic qualities are difficult to express. We know what we like when we see something, but defining that quality beforehand is nearly impossible. In nature, an object's beauty seems to lie in the intrinsic manifestation of its functions. For example, the delicate and colorful parts of a flower are not merely arbitrary visual patterns, but gain relevance as expressions of the flower's functional need to attract bees for the process of reproduction. The plant's distinctive appearance is an expression, in the most direct and essential way, of its functional needs. In nature, this integration between an object's function and appearance seems universal. So, for me, the foundation for visually pleasing and distinctive architecture grows out of a similar, direct and genuine desire to express visually the functions a building is intending to provide.

Form does follow function. Yet, in addition, for any work to be visually pleasing, it must not only be comprehensible, but also stimulating. There seems to be a continuum in the degree of visual complexity that is appropriate for a work of architecture. That continuum ranges from the most simple and ordered on one end, to the extremely complex and energetic on the other. I try to place my work, be it architecture, painting or sculpture, within that continuum. I try to balance simplicity, order, and coherence on one hand, with variety, complexity, and vitality on the other. If I move too far in one direction and my work becomes too regular, too ordered, too predictable or reminiscent, there is a sameness that becomes boring and monotonous. If I move too far in the other direction, too much diversity, too much novelty, or unpredictability, it can become uncommunicative, confusing and chaotic. There is a critical balance needed that is both coherent yet dynamic, both ordered yet delightful.

4. Social Responsibility

A good building is not only visually appealing, but is socially responsible. It is one that achieves its desired purposes using the least possible resources. It should strive to be cost-effective and to achieve maximum benefits with the least waste and unnecessary effort, always cognizant of the need to conserve energy and sustain and preserve our natural resources.

THE SEARCH FOR SPACE AND FORM: Creating Architecture

> All architecture is shelter, all great architecture is the design of space that contains cuddles, exalts or stimulates the persons in that space.
>
> Philip Johnson

With a sufficient understanding of my client's preferences, and a sense of the amenities and constraints of the site, I began the process of creating space and its enclosing form. The design of a home is a complex problem. Hundreds of issues need to be resolved. Looking back over the process, I seemed to have grappled with this complexity by breaking down the problem into smaller sub-problems, where fewer variables could be more readily comprehended and manipulated. I attacked these sub-problems through a series of drawings, which explored and tested solutions. The process started out abstract and global but, as components were resolved, became more specific and detailed. I produced a series of tracing paper overlay sketches in which an initial abstract diagram was transformed into a three-dimensional solution. Each drawing was a refinement of preceding ones. Each recorded my current understanding of the problem and proposed a partial solution, which was then tested against how well it would meet the objectives defined in the program, and my own desires for good architecture. Each new issue was exposed, then addressed and tentatively solved in the following sketches.

These tracing paper overlay drawings were a series of refinements (although, sometimes, they led to a completely new direction), which helped organize and prioritize the elements of the work. Some of the improvements shaped by this process, adding richness and subtlety to the final design, were: functional improvements, more appropriate volumetric and spatial arrangements and proportions, better definition of vistas and incorporation of sunlight, more meaningful arrangement of walls and openings, a better relationship to the land, and easier constructability.

The expression of the house was generated through a dialogue between internal and external influences. I continually worked back and forth resolving conflicts between the spatial needs on the inside of the house and the form expression of that space on the outside. My overriding goal was to design a special place, one that would fit my client's lifestyle and which would respond to, and express, the unique nature of their site.

The following sketches illustrate the process of generating space and form.

The site for this house is an open field on the north-facing slope of a mountain (Figure 2). From this elevated location, there are outstanding panoramic views over the surrounding countryside and long vistas to distant mountains.

I began the process by responding to the program and the site. Information from the program was converted into an abstract 'circulation diagram' (Figure 3) that enabled me to examine, comprehend and establish general relationships between spaces and their connection to the site. The diagram was a useful way to describe and understand the relative position of each space and the connections between them, and to account for the impact of external conditions on their location. To the extent that I understood how each space functioned, I located it in a position that seemed appropriate to its needs. Spaces were positioned to achieve a logical circulation flow between them, with an appropriate separation of private spaces from public ones, and an orientation that took advantage of sunlight and views. As I organized the diagram, I also tried to be mindful of the site's constraints, such as the location of buildable areas, property line setbacks, topography, wind direction (to locate protected outdoor living areas), and the location and proximity of adjacent pedestrian and vehicular access ways. From previous site visits, I had identified two site locations that seemed most appropriate based on topography, views, adjacency to an existing garage/guest cottage, and sun orientation. I had these two locations in mind as I manipulated the diagram.

Although abstract, this diagram set down basic spatial relationships and implied, through the abstraction of connecting lines, where there would be required additional transitional spaces not listed in the program, such as foyers, hallways, galleries, entries and vestibules. Once I was comfortable with the logic of the diagram, I needed to transform it into a scaled drawing, as the actual size and proportion of spaces topologically affects their arrangement. Some alternative plans (see Figures 4 and 5) were laid out, with spaces positioned using the relationships in the diagram as a guide. Spaces were sized and proportioned in a rough attempt to accommodate basic activities, knowing that they would be developed and refined later into more livable and comfortable places.

As I proceeded, I reconsidered each of the activities being contemplated. Who would participate in the activities? How would the participants move about? From where would they come? Where would they go? What furniture, fixtures and equipment would be required? Where should they be located? How much space would they need? Tentatively, I sketched some furniture locations to test whether preliminary room configurations would be adequate,

Figure 2 View from the site looking north

wall surfaces sufficient, and overall proportions appropriate. Since most furniture is made to fit straight walls and rectangular configurations, I started with rectangular shaped spaces and laid out the spaces orthogonally. Once I had a better comprehension of issues, I knew I would be able to try other configurations. I thought about enclosing surfaces. How opaque or transparent should they be? In addition, people need to move about logically, so I positioned spaces for easy connectivity with other spaces and I defined each one to ensure unimpeded movement within.

When initially configuring these spaces, I was especially mindful of the direction of sunlight and views. Although pleasing views were desirable everywhere, due to functional and topological considerations, it was impossible to incorporate the best view from every room. Some prioritizing or compromise was necessary—I favored more heavily used spaces. Paradoxically, the restriction of not being able to take advantage of views from every room resulted in a more innovative and creative organization as I attempted to overcome this constraint. I find this irony an important aspect of the creative process. The very fact that I was unable to achieve an objective working in a conventional way, led to more interesting, unconventional ways to overcome the limitation.

It is generally an amenity when views face toward the south because glass walls that take advantage of the views also benefit from friendly southern exposure. In this house, the expansive views were northerly, facing away from the southern sun. In developing the design, the spatial arrangement and form of the house evolved, as spaces with northerly views were arranged to allow south-facing openings to capture sunlight. This elongated arrangement enabled natural cross ventilation, as well as secondary views back up the mountain, and resulted in a house more expressive of its location.

As I proceeded to lay out spaces, I considered how people would move through them. I thought three-dimensionally. That is, although I drew a two-dimensional plan, I tried to understand its implications in three dimensions. I virtually 'walked' through the spaces, trying to imagine what I would see as I moved around, frequently testing my assumptions by making sketches to verify them. I worked back and forth between spaces—resolving conflicts and maximizing objectives. Initially, my intent was to establish good utilitarian relationships, ensuring that activities would function properly. Once something worked, I searched for more innovative and appealing ways to enclose the space and express its form.

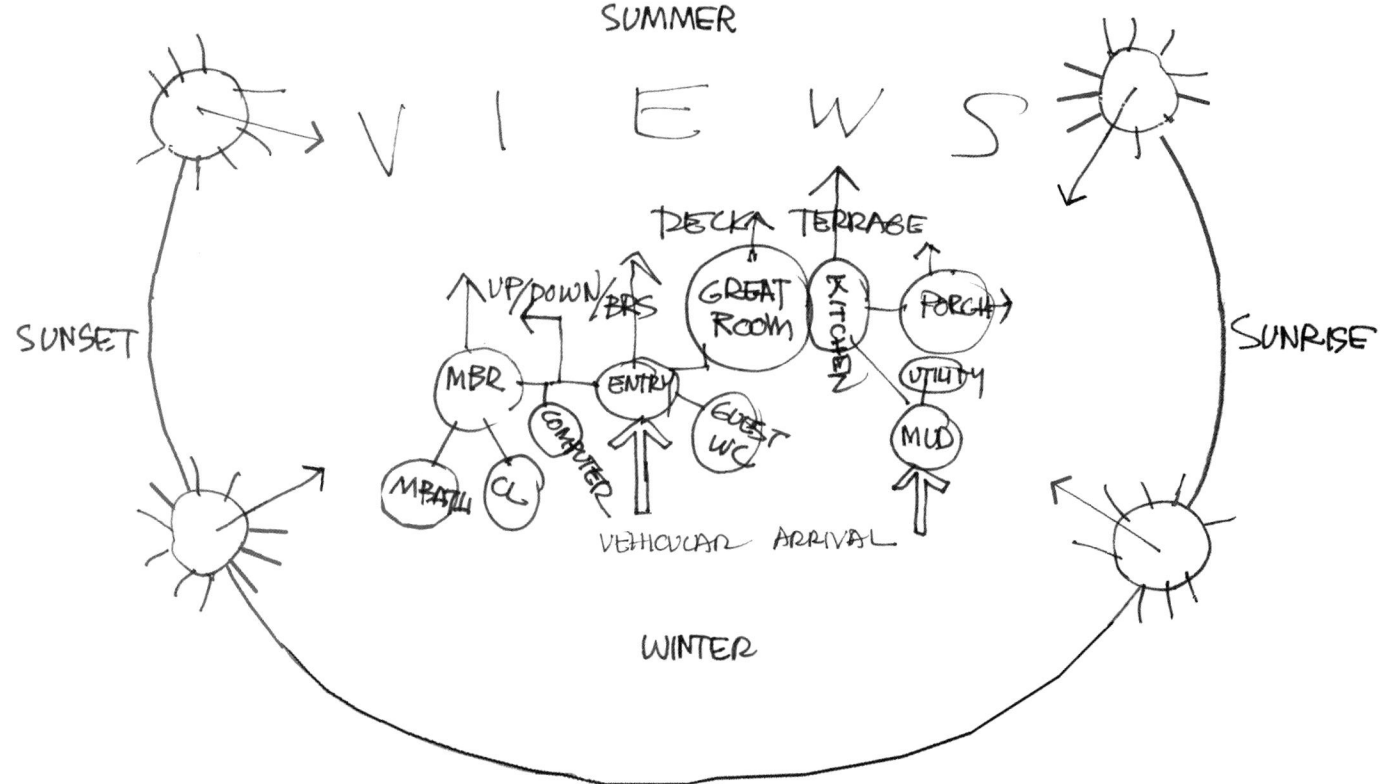

Figure 3 Circulation diagram showing relationship between spaces, views and the sun

The same psychological need to find order in our surroundings seemed to drive the design process. Throughout, I constantly sought to discern some overriding idea around which to compose and organize the seemingly disparate parts of the solution. Sometimes an idea emerged suddenly ("Eureka!"), triggered by some connection to a past experience. Other times, it would reveal itself slowly, developing "like an image on photographic paper," as physicist Peter Caruthers once so aptly observed.

When I first visited the site for this house I was intrigued by the dilapidated remains of a former residence that sat where the new house might be located. I recall exploring the partially remaining structure, feeling as if I was on the edge of a cliff gazing out at distant mountains. No foreground barriers hindered my panoramic view. Achieving the quality of that unconstrained view became a motivating incentive as I tried to recreate that same opportunity in the layout of the new house. These 'gut' images are meaningful and it's easy to be seduced by them. But they may limit the discovery of other more creative or appropriate ideas prematurely. It takes an effort to seek other alternatives and I try to take a cue from brainstorming. Initially, I strive to be open to ideas and to generate a variety of alternatives. At first, I am not too critical (some seemingly poor ideas can trigger good ones). Later, when I have a greater understanding of the problem, I can be more discriminating and rule out alternatives that seem inappropriate.

To begin with, I tried to establish a clear spatial organization for the house. Previous experience helped me formulate appropriate solutions, but this was a search—a process of trial and error. Each sketch uncovered some new issue that needed to be addressed.

The configurations of these preliminary floor plans were influenced by the following considerations: what should be the appropriate size and proportion of each space? How should these configurations relate to one another to allow direct, unencumbered movement between and through them? How could the spatial organization be clearly expressed and still provide spatial variety and interest? How could private areas be separated from public ones to provide acoustic and visual privacy? How should entrances be expressed? What were the most favorable locations for ingress and access to the outside? What should be the relationship between floors? Where and how should stairs be located to make gracious and efficient connections? How could views be maximized and spaces oriented for access to sunlight? Figures 4 and 5 show an initial attempt to address these parameters.

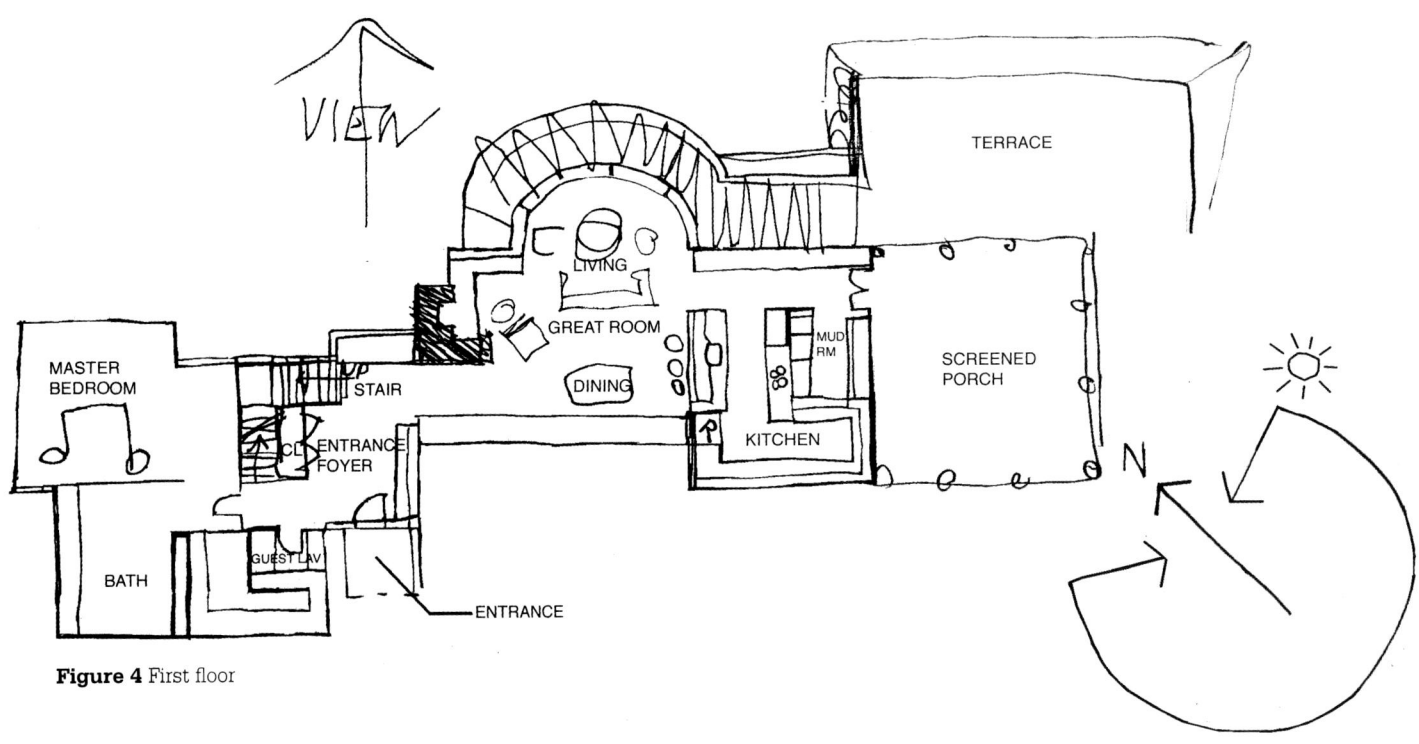

Figure 4 First floor

Figure 4

This sketch was my first attempt to convert the abstract circulation diagram (Figure 3) into a floor plan with real spaces (room labels have been added to the original drawings for clarity). An entrance was drawn (a dotted line indicated a protective roof). The entrance was particularly important because it was the logical starting point for laying out the house. It was the transition between activities within the house and the more public outside world. Inside, a foyer would be a place to pause, to greet people, remove a coat and have the opportunity to reorient oneself to a new environment.

Eventually, the entrance's size, its scale, degree of formality, ease of access, clear identity, expression of comfort, sense of security, and its connection to the site, would begin to establish an overall image for the house. Initially, the desire was simply to create an arrival place that was easily identifiable but not pretentious—one that afforded protection from inclement weather and was large enough to accommodate several people comfortably. On the inside, the entrance was a transitional space. There is an indication of a stair leading to upper and lower levels. The more public and active areas of living, dining and kitchen were shown zoned to the right side of the plan. The more private spaces, the master bedroom and its accessory spaces, and stairs to other bedrooms, were to the left.

As I sketched, I was quite aware of the steep slope of the land. I knew I needed to find ways to accommodate and take advantage of the slope using terraces and decks. A screened porch and terrace were positioned on the southern right side of the plan to take advantage of the sun and to connect to the activities of the kitchen. A deck led from living area to terrace, while a semi-circular bay tried to capture and express the panoramic view from the living area.

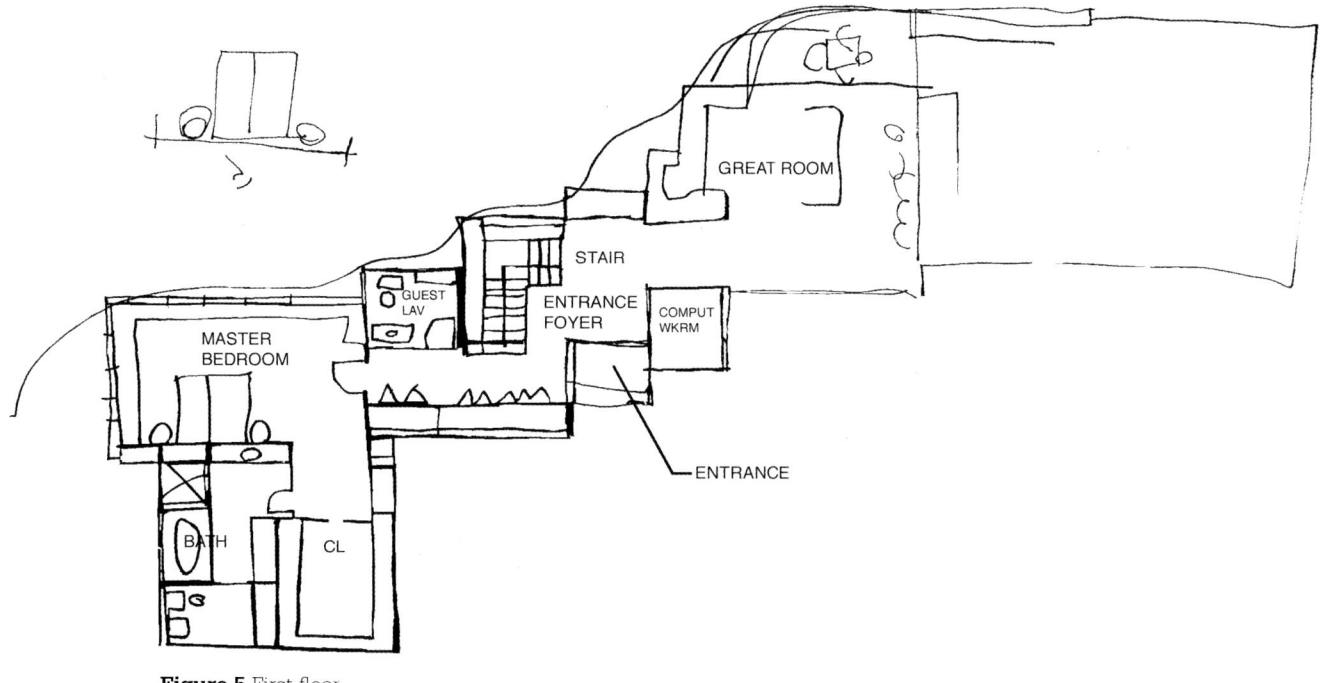

Figure 5 First floor

Figure 5

Here, I tried pulling the master bedroom back to the uphill side of the site to afford a closer relationship to the sloping grade. Perhaps there would be the opportunity for direct-grade access from the master bedroom. The L-shape of this plan began to suggest the potential for a protected outdoor space adjacent to the entrance that could be an orienting place for those arriving by car. This plan explored a series of offsets where spaces were arranged so that corners could be opened with glass to optimize the extraordinary views. Furniture indications helped define the size and proportion of spaces. For example, the sketch in the upper left of the figure verified the wall surface needed for a master bed and side tables. These early sketches were exercises in understanding the topological relationship between spaces. That is, how does the size and proportion of a space fit with that of another to produce appropriate spatial relationships and pleasing form? These initial studies quickly revealed that a deeper understanding of specific components of the house would be needed before an overall plan could be advanced. I started to focus only on the master bedroom and its attendant spaces: entrance, dressing and bath (see Figures 6 and 7).

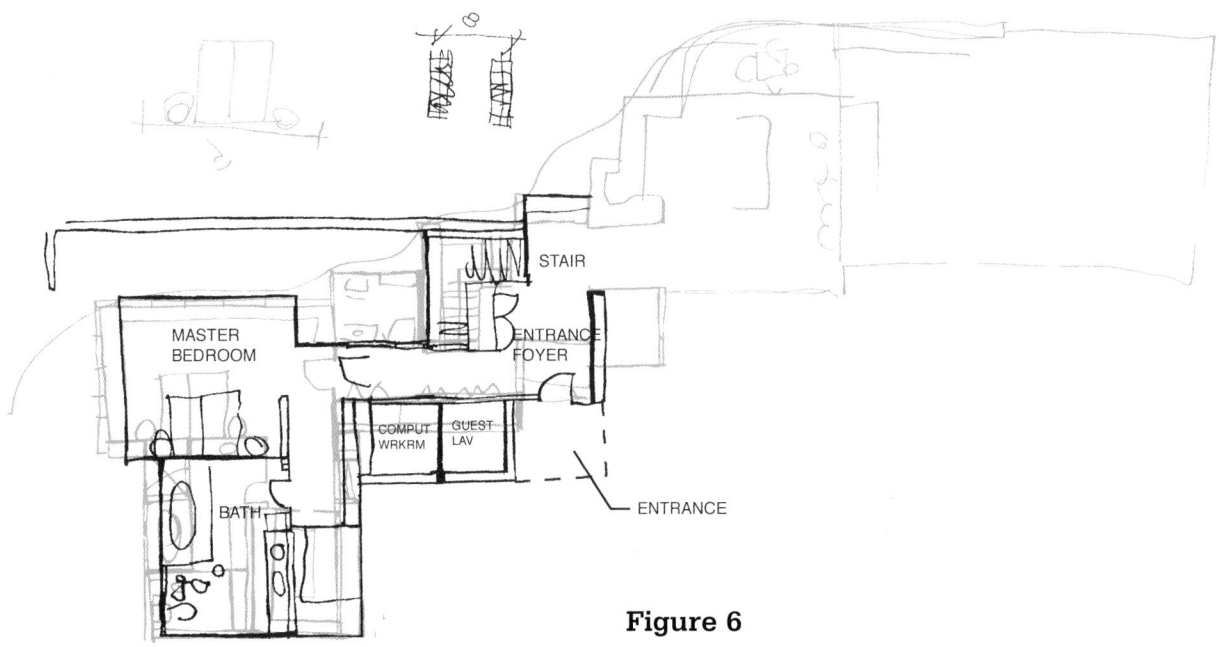

Figure 6 First floor

Figure 6

In this overlay of the previous sketch (the overlay drawing is shown in black, the previous sketch [Figure 5], in gray), the master bedroom was again pulled back for possible terrace access, but projected outward to take advantage of the panoramic view. Beyond the master bedroom, a retaining wall indicated the potential for a private outdoor terrace.

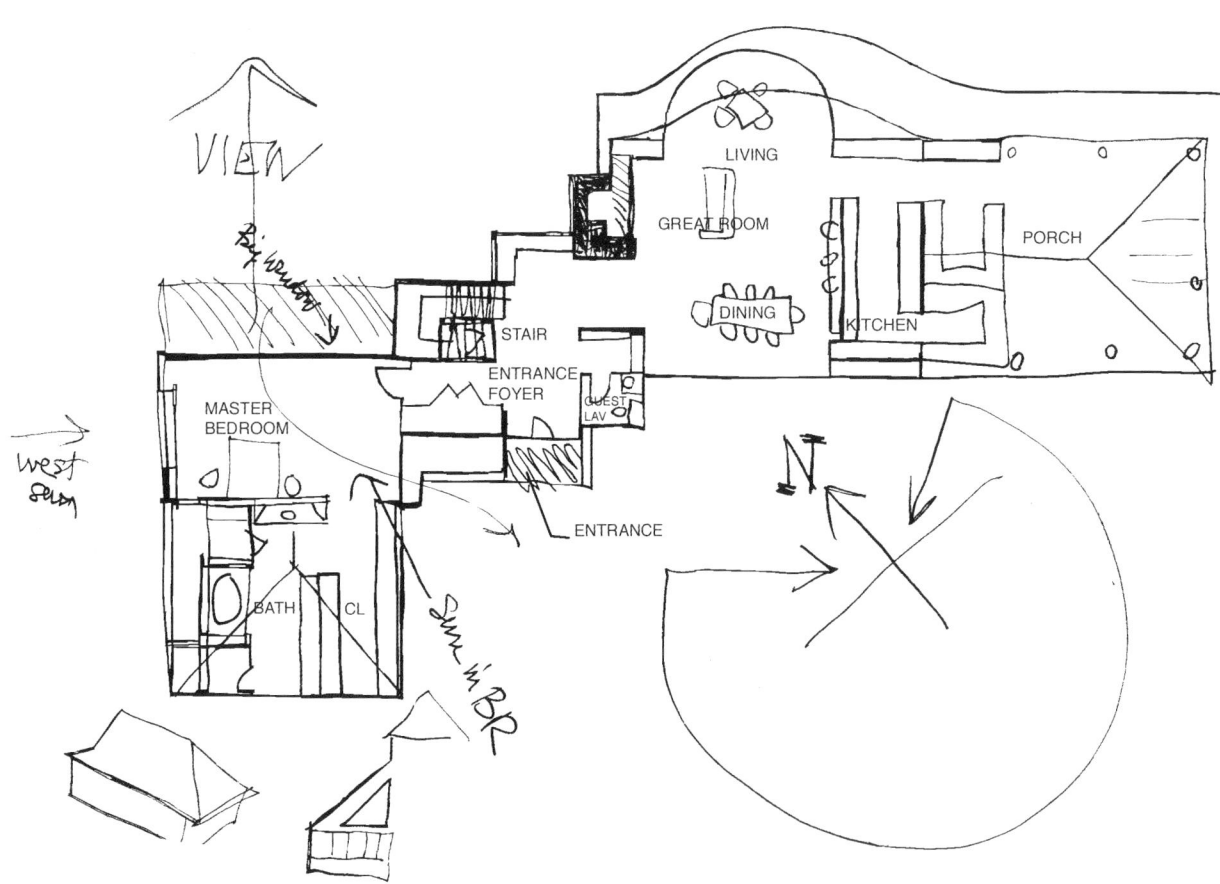

Figure 7 First floor

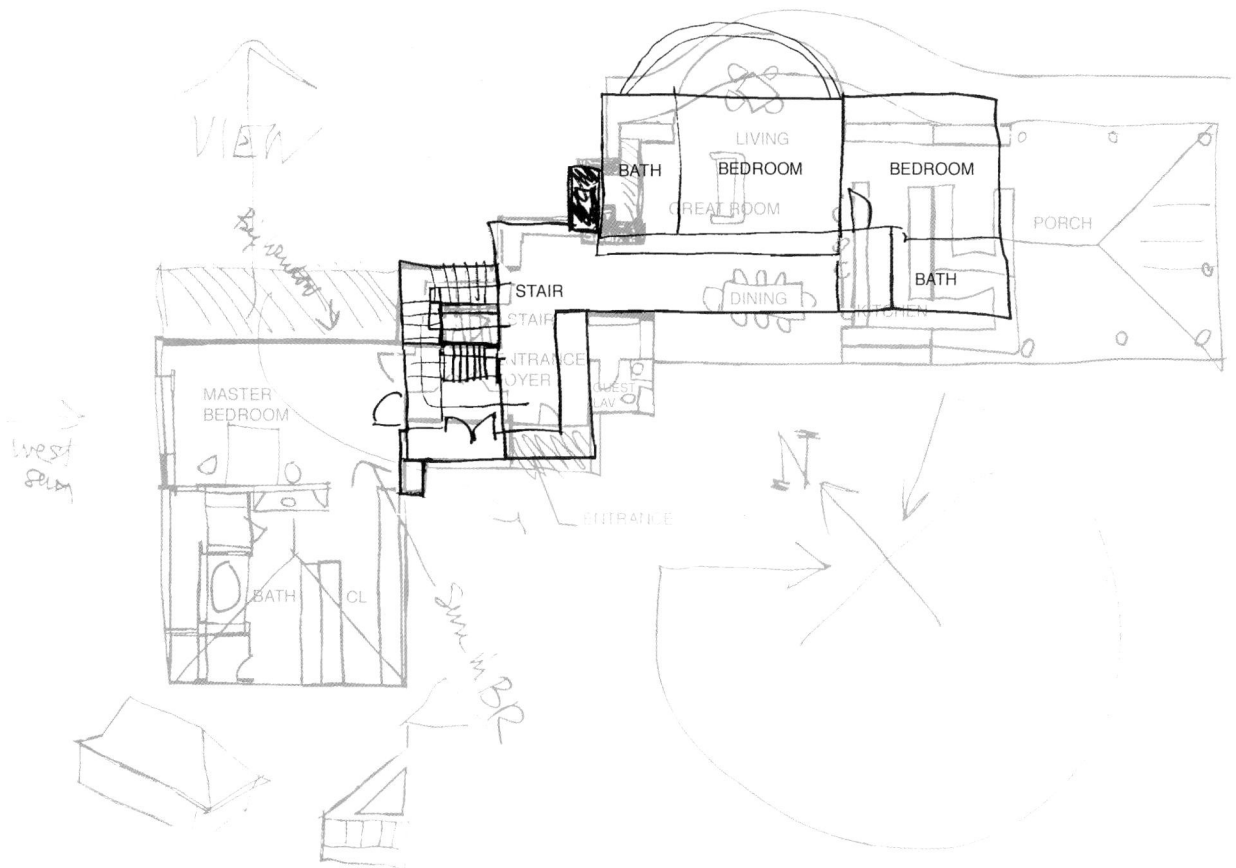

Figure 8 Second floor

Figure 7

In this layout, I considered making the master bedroom a simpler, less articulated space with an extended deck. In this option, the grand view would be reserved for the more active great room, with a curving glass wall to capture the far-reaching vista. Initially, I indicated two spatial conceptions for the great room. One separated the living areas from the kitchen, the other incorporated the kitchen as part of a single, integrated living space. The guest lavatory was flipped to the right side of the entrance, keeping guests further away from the private area of the master bedroom. Concern over the lack of sunlight in the north-facing master bedroom led to a series of sketches exploring the possibility of manipulating the roof to catch the southern light. But, before trying that, I needed to confirm that no space was needed above the master bedroom for program requirements.

Figure 8

This is a diagrammatic layout of the second floor, which was used to test its relationship to the floor below. It confirmed that bedrooms and bathrooms could be accommodated on this level without the need to impact the master bedroom. Two bedrooms were shown. The other two bedrooms required could be located below, on the 'walk out' side of the ground (lowest) floor. This diagram demonstrated that manipulation and reworking of the two floor plans would be necessary to enable them to stack appropriately. For example, the stair needed to function properly at all floors. Safety, ease of movement, the width and length of run, tread-to-riser proportions, and visual expression would all affect stair design. But, at this early stage, the most important matter was to ensure that where one started up on the first floor, and where one arrived at the second, enabled the logical functioning of each floor plan. A 4-foot-wide stair was sketched (a comfortable width based on previous experience). An approximate, overall length of the stair was calculated by multiplying the number of treads by their depth. Floor-to-floor heights determine the number of stair risers and their accompanying treads. Initial assumptions were made about appropriate ceiling heights and depths of floor structure in order to calculate the area needed for the stair.

Figure 9
Now knowing that the zone above the master bedroom could be free from program requirements, I returned to determining the master bedroom area. This sketch further explored the idea of clerestory windows. Aside from catching south light, the high windows could also serve as a 'chimney' to naturally ventilate the master bedroom.

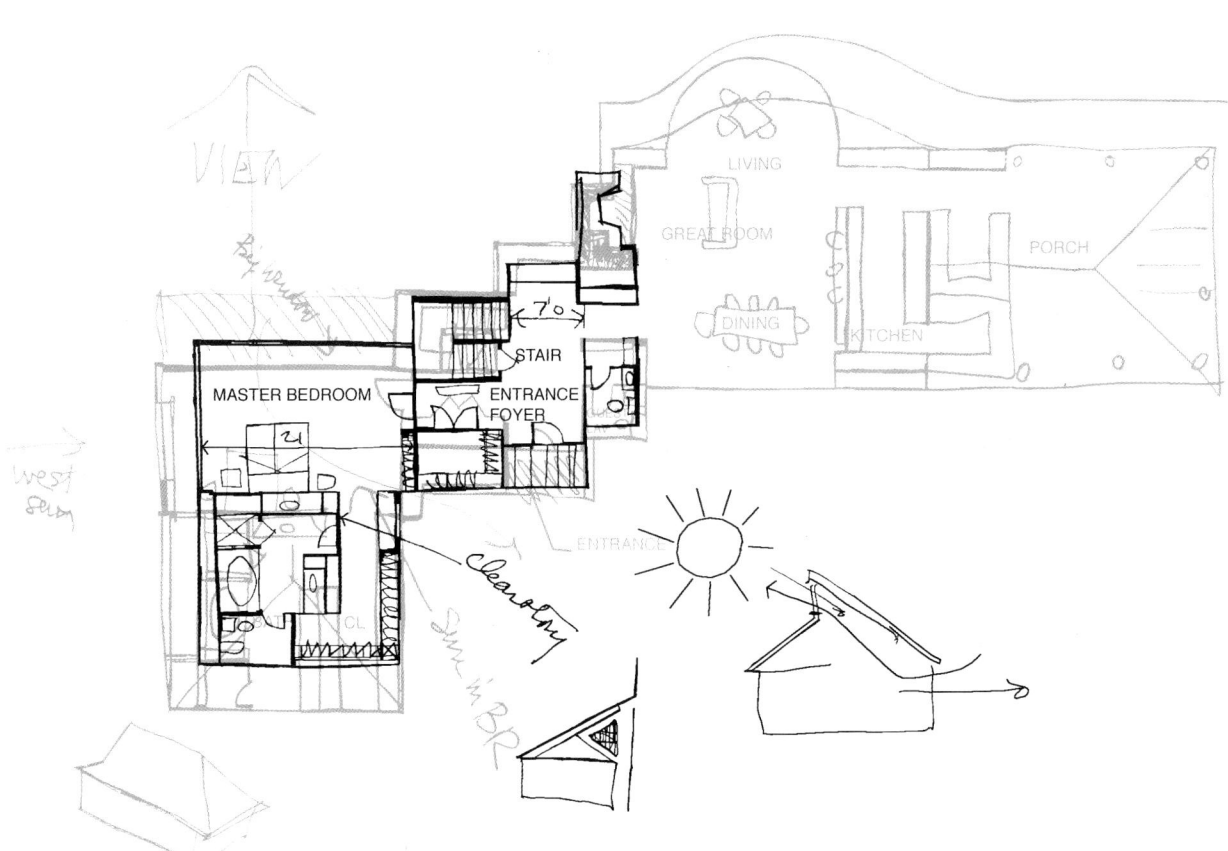

Figure 9 First floor

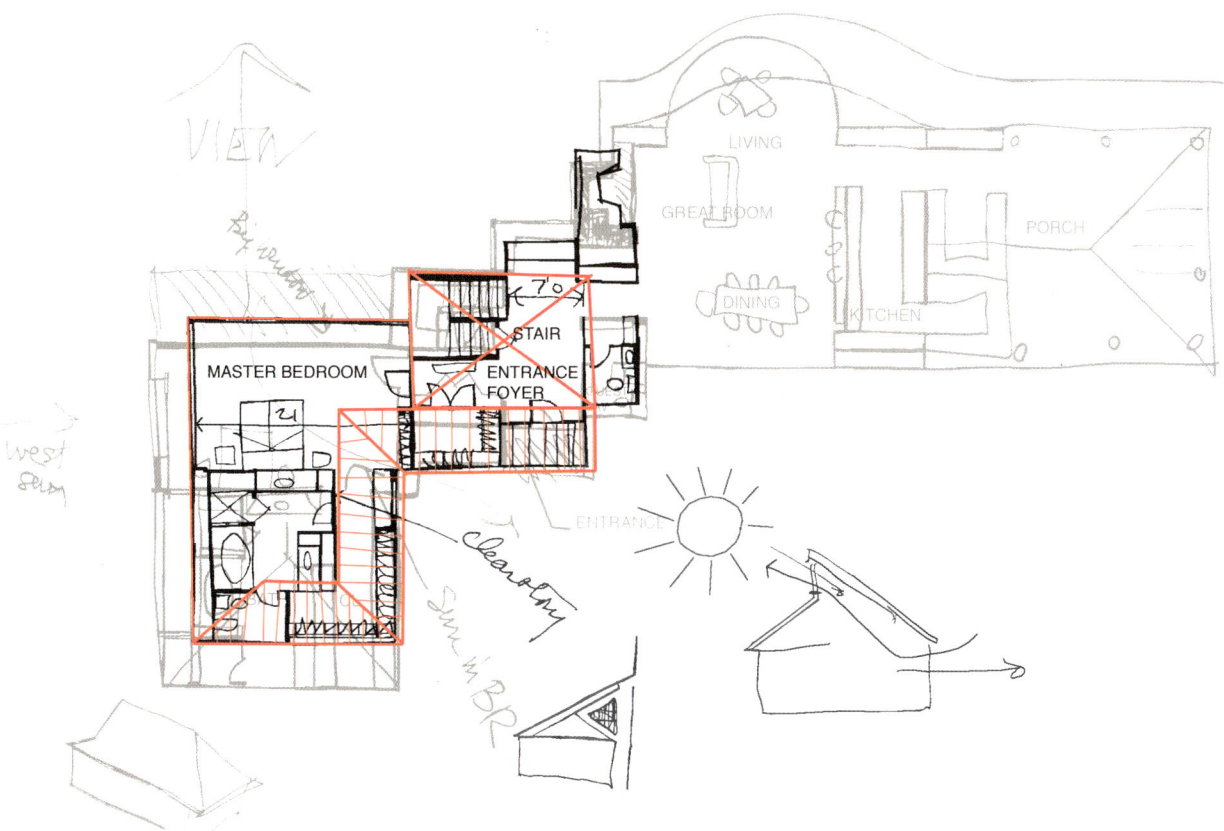

Figure 10 First floor

Figure 10

The roof, especially a sloping one dictated by climatic conditions in the northeast, significantly influences the sculptural form of a house. The search for, and testing of, an appropriate roof expression (shown in red) followed closely the development of the floor plans. There was a need to create a rational roof shape, where ridges, eaves, slopes and intersections were arranged to produce simple, watertight intersections and positive drainage. Simultaneously, there was the desire to reinforce the clarity of the floor plan, by expressing on the exterior the volume and organization of spaces within. In addition, the manipulation of eave height and overhang reduced the house's scale to convey a pleasing form and feeling of protective shelter.

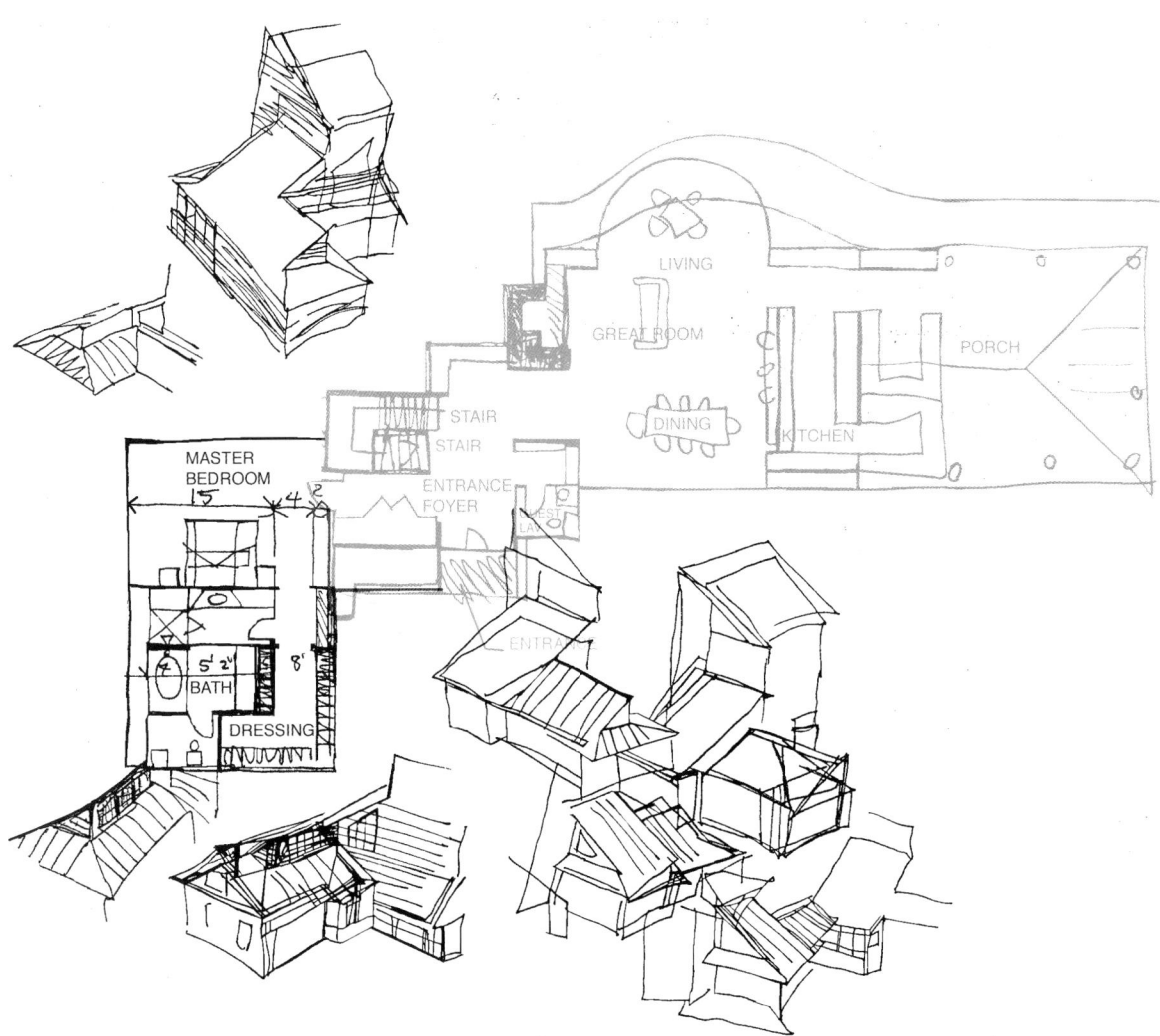

Figure 11 First floor

Figure 11

At this point, I had no idea what an appropriate expression for the house might be. The idea of the roof opening up to capture sunlight, and the simultaneous potential such a possibility presented for cross ventilation, suggested the beginnings of a form. These sketches explored that possibility. Not having the need for programmed space above the master bedroom ensured privacy and acoustic separation. Equally, this arrangement augured a more interesting expression, as the space under the pitched roof could be incorporated into the volume of the bedroom ceiling. Later in the process, to be more cost-effective, some of that underutilized volume became a mezzanine for a computer workspace (see Figure 29, second floor).

The height of the house was limited by zoning, but a space set high above the ground, to take maximum advantage of the panoramic views, seemed a favorable place for the 'quiet room' my clients desired. It could be logically positioned as an upper extension of the central stair. The 'tower' could also help ventilate the home, cooling the house in the summer by venting warmer air out and allowing cooler air to be drawn in below. These sketches began to reflect that dynamic. They sought an appropriate roof form for the master bedroom and explored how that form might integrate with a higher 'tower' mass. These drawings—images of shed roofs—sparked thoughts of rural mountain structures, and buildings made of utilitarian forms and materials. For this vacation house, a simple, direct, vernacular expression seemed worth pursuing and became an important influence as the design evolved.

All of the figures reproduced in this book were drawn by hand on transparent tracing paper. This technique allowed me to see and sketch over previous illustrations. Unexpected relationships between my new sketches and underlying ones often triggered otherwise unnoticed connections. This unpredictability was useful in generating ideas. As I write, existing building modeling software such as Google SketchUp and Revit are being developed and improved. These programs have become extremely helpful tools for testing and evaluating alternatives once they are generated but, so far, I have been unable to duplicate on the computer the unexpected spontaneity that is enabled by drawing directly onto tracing paper overlays. Perhaps technological advances in software will one day accommodate this advantage.

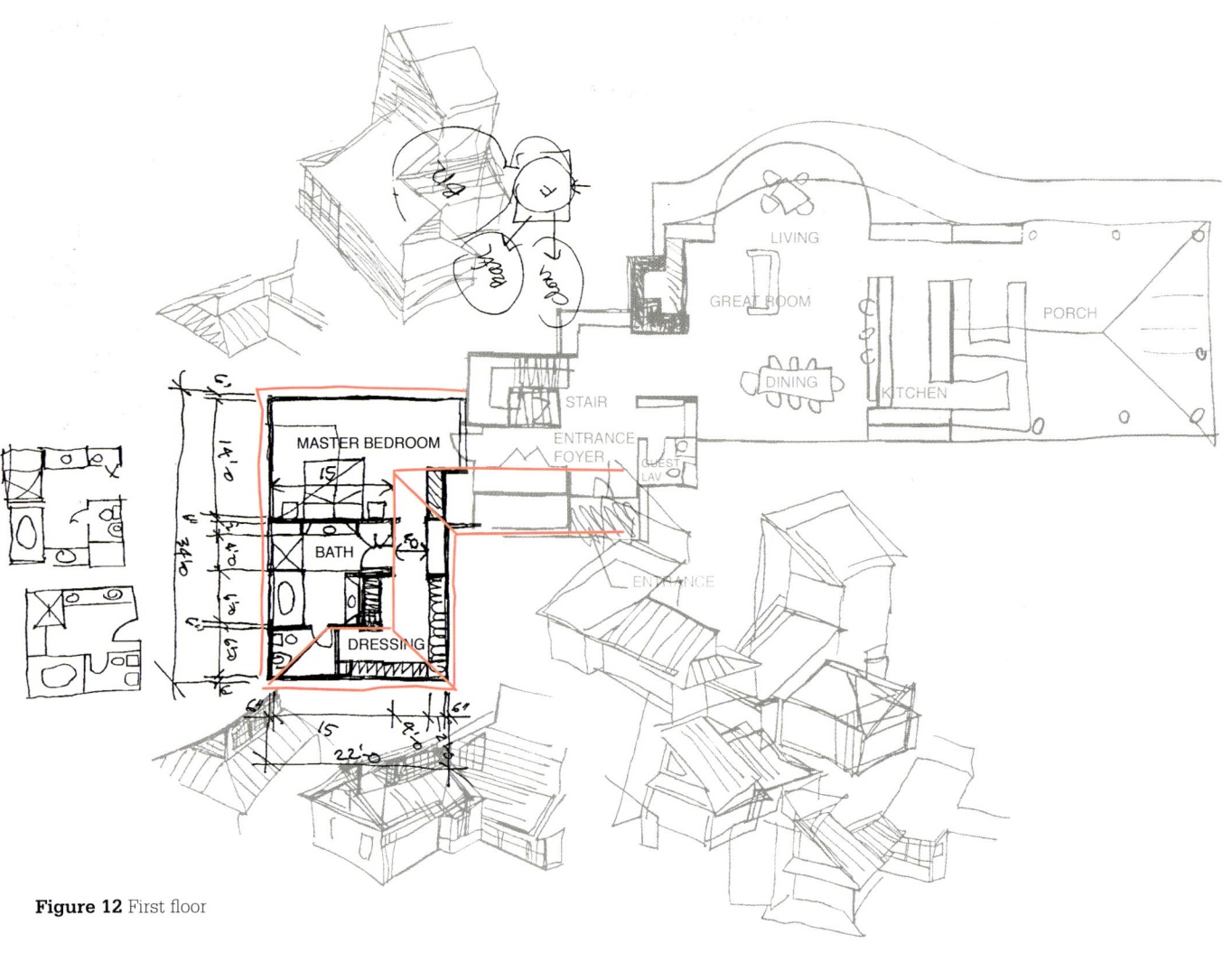

Figure 12 First floor

Figure 12

In completing this overlay, I was, for the moment, comfortable with my understanding of the master bedroom. This plan provided the necessary space and could be satisfactorily developed into a gracious yet functional master suite, so I added critical dimensions to confirm its size. On a positive budgetary note, the master bedroom area was slightly smaller than I had estimated in the original program (see page 12). I began to illustrate a possible roof shape and form for this area, and hoped that further development of the second floor and its roof would confirm that this preliminary massing was appropriate.

Figure 13

I laid out the second floor more definitively than before, positioning the stairs in relation to the floor below, and indicating an extension of the stair leading to the tower 'quiet room'. Clearly, the smaller, second floor program would not fit neatly over the larger floor plate below. To accommodate this difference, I considered a one-story section along the uphill side of the house. This lower mass resolved the programmatic difference between floors and would create, in a positive way, an appropriately scaled, smaller element on the entrance side of the house. Many of the following sketches, searching for an appropriate form, deal with resolving the dichotomy between floors and the relationship between floors and roof. In working out these differences, I considered how structural loads could be carried and logically transferred to the ground. The flow of circulation from one floor to another had to work smoothly, and the form of the house and its spaces needed to be unified and, hopefully, to appear, 'predestined'.

Noted in this sketch was the difficulty of covering a semi-circular shape (the great room extension) with a pitched roof. Here, instead of a roof, I tried making the semi-circular area a roof deck or porch. But access to the deck seemed odd and privacy for the bedrooms was compromised. I needed a more workable solution.

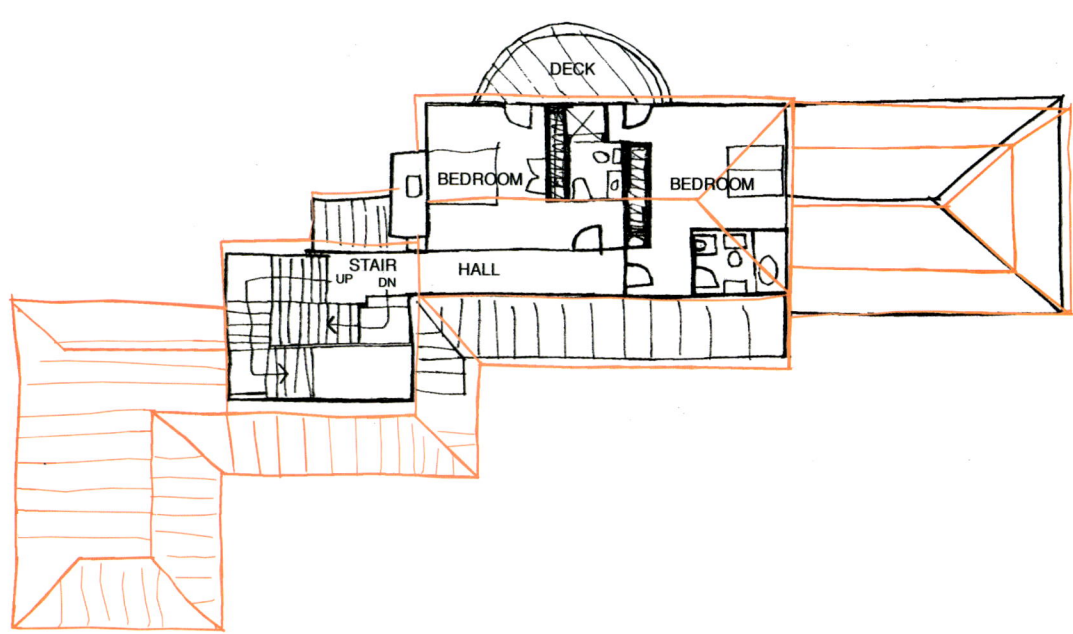

Figure 13 Second floor

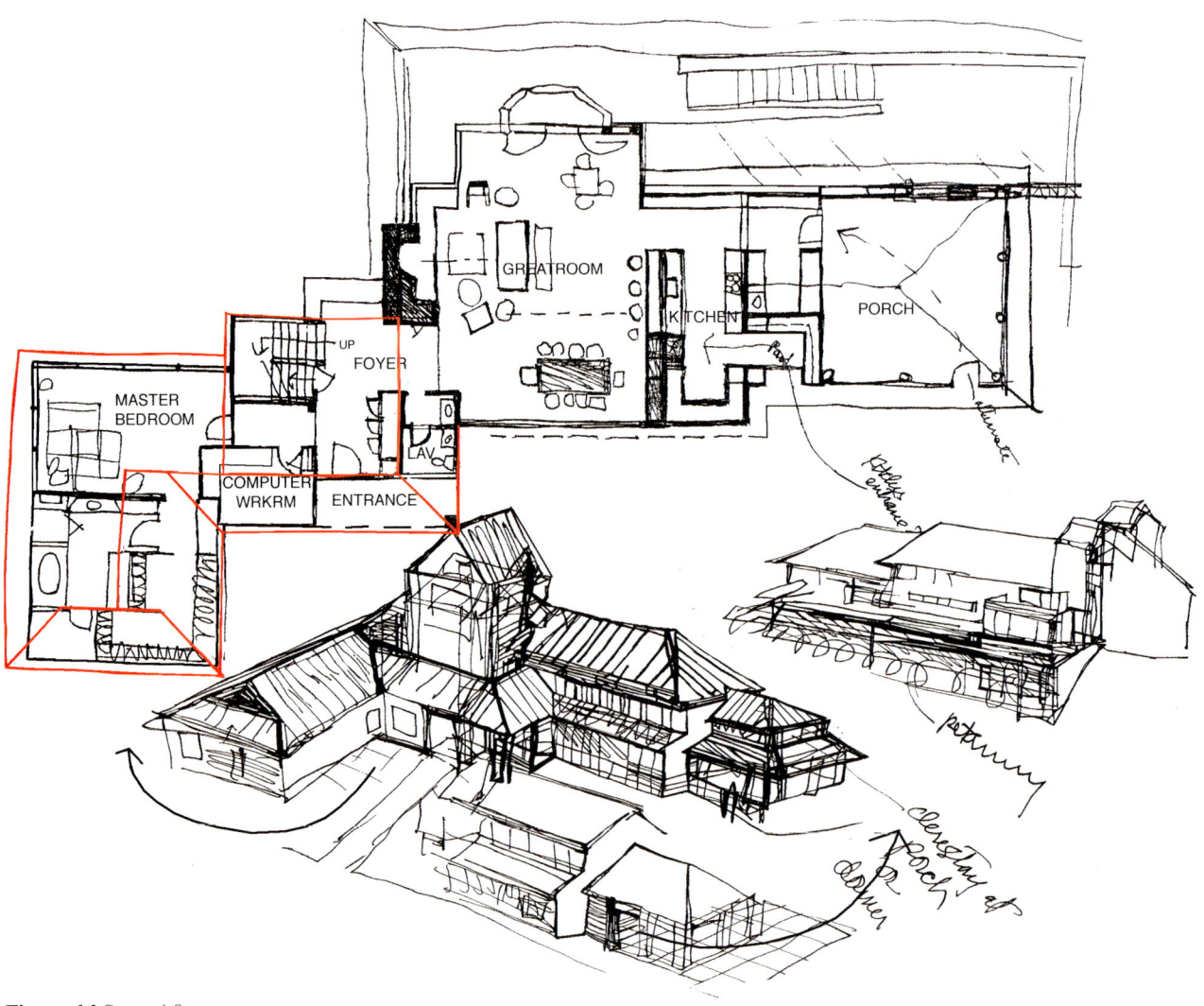

Figure 14 Second floor

Figure 14

I redrew the entire first floor plan to integrate the knowledge I had gained from previous drawings. Along with the plan, I drew sketches trying to show how the plan might be expressed in three dimensions. The inside and outside needed to work harmoniously, so when exterior expressions seemed problematic, I changed the plan to mitigate these conditions. Alternatively, if the plan could not change, I explored other ways of modeling the exterior. Initial thoughts on massing led to expressing the central portion of the house as a higher element—stepping down to surrounding lower-scaled components. The goal for this vacation 'cottage' was an informal residential scale, so I reduced the apparent size of the house by emphasizing a one-story eave height. Again, I thought about the L-shaped layout with its extended arm. Perhaps I could supplement this configuration with the rising topography of the mountain adjacent to the house, to help create a semi-protected arrival space. This space might be developed to mediate the transition from the open, undeveloped natural landscape of the surrounding mountainside, to the secluded, intimate, human-scaled environment of the house.

Stepped roof forms could help mitigate the overall size of the house by articulating smaller scaled pieces. The tower, rising vertically from the center of the house, vicariously implied the outstanding views from within and added variety to the massing. The visually important tower was a marker identifying the location of the main entrance. Noted on this sketch are arrows indicating drainage flow. Proper drainage is an important consideration for any house, but especially for this mountain location where melting snows would generate extensive run-off.

Figure 15

The configuration of the first floor plan (Figure 14) established a tentative exterior boundary for the ground floor below. The exterior wall of the ground floor would become the foundation wall for the house. This sketch, an exploratory layout of the ground floor, confirms that within this area, space was available for the program's two bedrooms, two baths, and mechanical space.

The sloping mountainside enabled the downhill side of the house to be above-grade, but an effort would be needed to ensure that the spatial quality and comfort of the bedrooms on this lowest level were equal to those on the upper floor. A scribbled sketch (shown upside-down in the upper right) probed the difficulties with placing the bedrooms on this level.

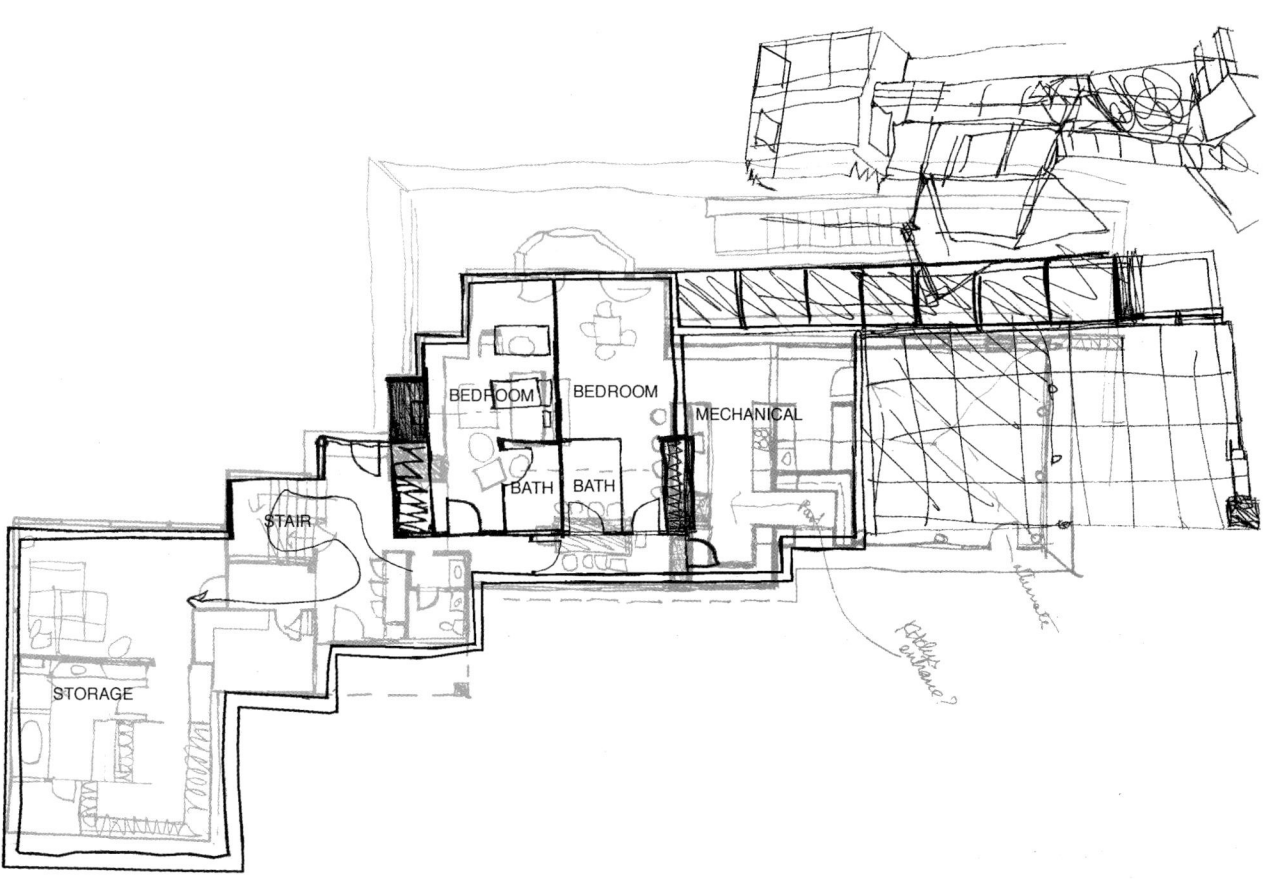

Figure 15 Ground floor

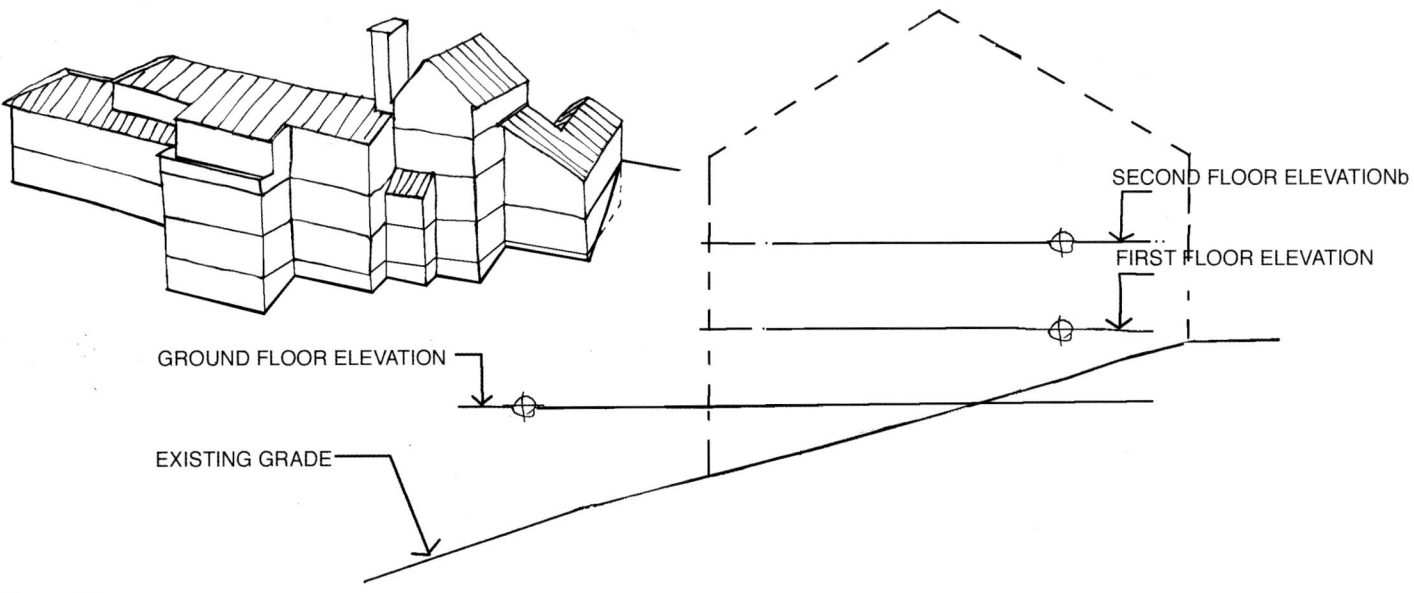

Figure 16

Figure 16

This sketch section expressed the relationship of the lowest (ground floor) bedrooms to the exterior grade. It was 'cut' at one of two site locations considered for the house. This location on the northwestern boundary of the property had good, long views, but a row of trees marking the edge of the property blocked the wide panoramic vistas. The advantage of this location was its proximity to an existing building, which housed a two-car garage and potential guest quarters. This sketch showed that it would be impossible, without an excessively high ground floor, to enter the house at grade on the first floor (south side) and have easy on-grade access at the ground level (north side) as well. The very steep grade (approximately 25 percent) and the trees limiting the panoramic view resulted in the selection of the other more central site location. Here, direct access to outside grade was less difficult and the view was unconstrained. My clients also favored this more central location even though its relationship to the existing guest cottage and garage was more distant.

Figures 17–18

Unease over the quality of bedrooms on the lowest level (ground floor) led to a series of studies that considered all four bedrooms on the second floor. These sketches show the development of that alternative. One option (Figure 17) tried using the space over the master bedroom. That was rejected in favor of space over the porch (Figure 18), ensuring privacy and acoustic separation for the master bedroom.

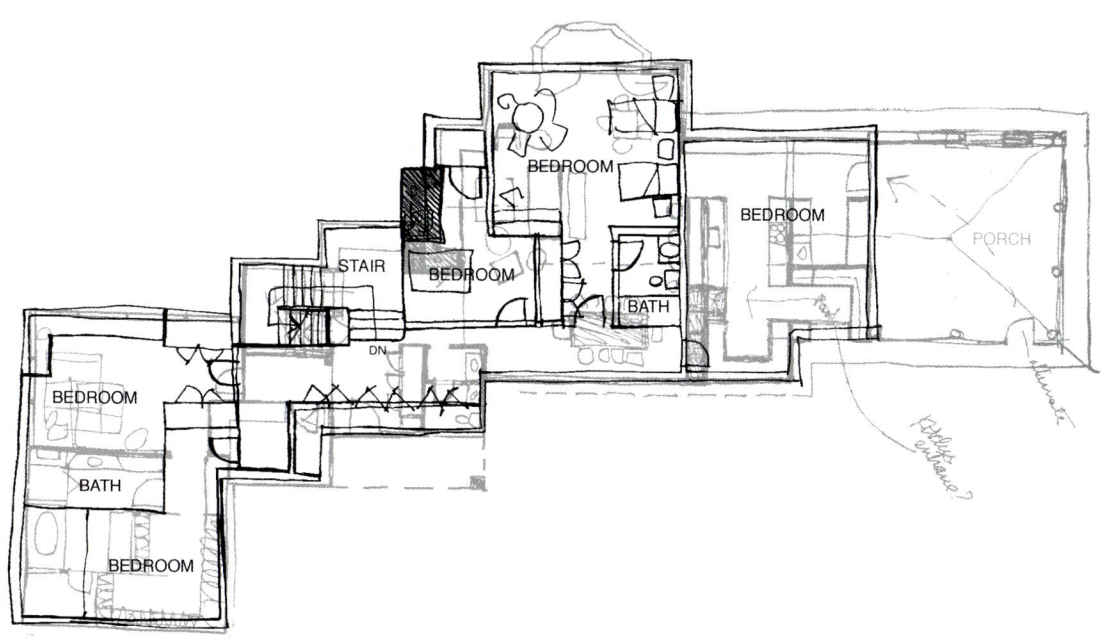

Figure 17 Second floor

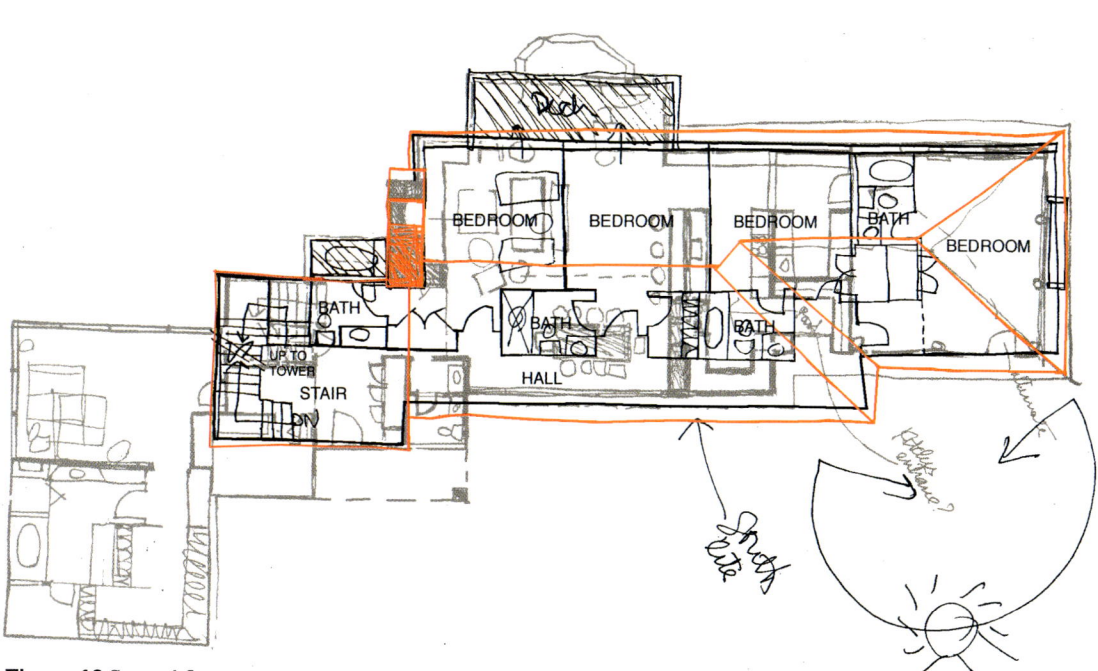

Figure 18 Second floor

Figure 19

With four bedrooms on the second floor, the two-story scale of the house seemed too large. An offset in the plan helped reduce the apparent size, but the two-story height was a concern. These sketches examined the house from the uphill, southern side. They showed possible development of the roof form and massing, and also indicated some initial thoughts about window placement. I needed to open up the south side of the house to capture sunlight in spaces where the primary views (and windows) would face north.

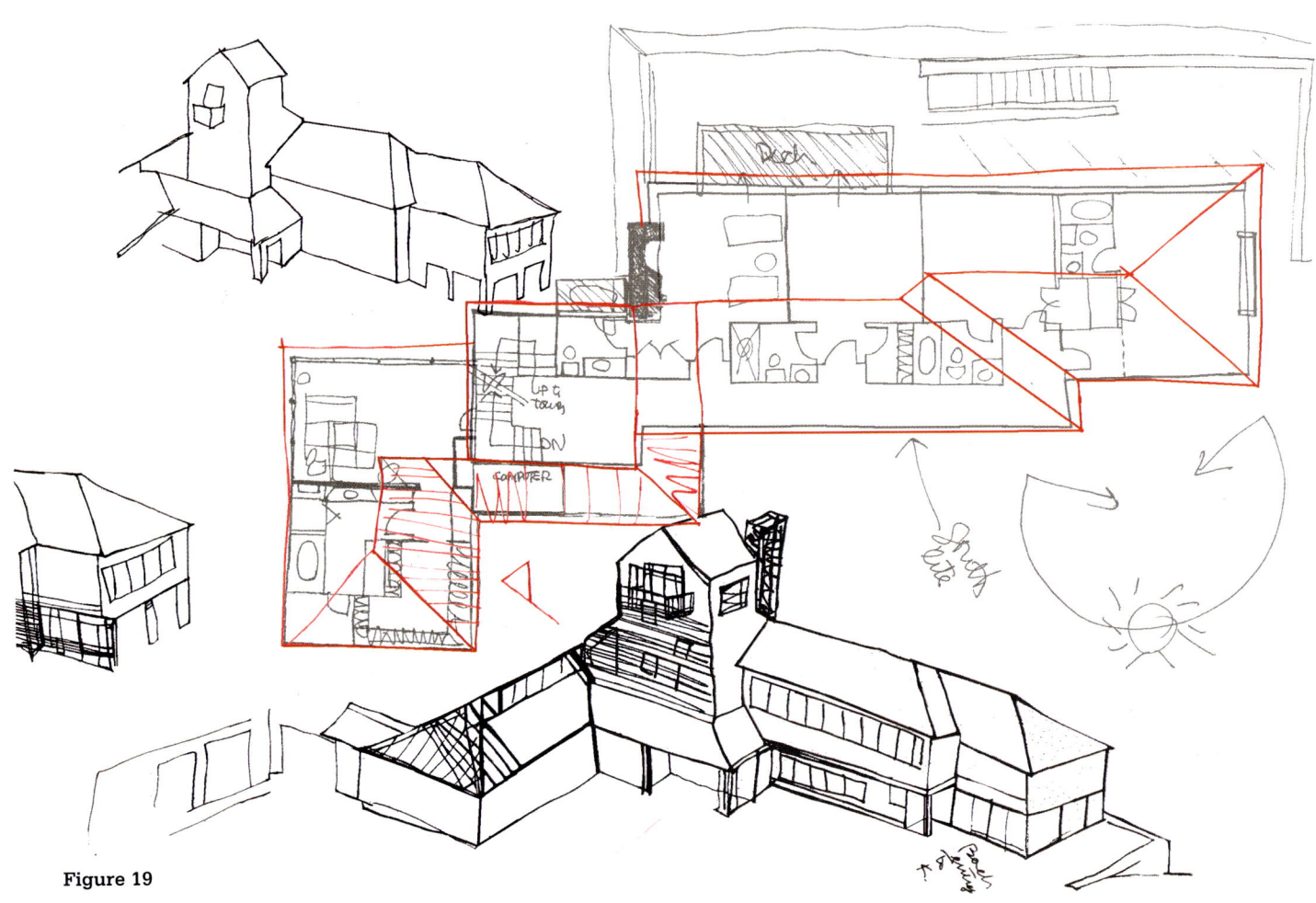

Figure 19

Figure 20

Additional sketches from the north, downhill side of the house considered how various massing options might be expressed, and the visual effect of having four bedrooms on the second floor. On early sketches, I had indicated a semi-circular configuration for the great room, but that form evolved into a simpler rectangular shape that was less pretentious, less expensive to build and easier to integrate into the overall building form. With these sketches, I also sought to find expression for my initial concept—to experience the scene from the great room windows as if one were standing on the edge of a precipice with no foreground railings or decks impeding the expansive view. But the pragmatic desire for immediate and adjacent outdoor living space, directly accessible from the great room, would later result in extending the space onto a projecting deck.

The design process for this project seemed to evolve in a non-linear way, which was like opening Pandora's box. Before I could solve one problem, or resolve one set of issues, new questions arose. In addressing these questions, still other uncertainties demanded attention. Intent on solving an immediate problem, I now understand that I was being led through a series of explorations (a decision tree) that ultimately exposed for me the full complexity of the situation. It wasn't until I had achieved an overall understanding of the problem that I had the knowledge to devise an appropriate solution and judge its quality.

Each new drawing presented a hypothesis to be evaluated. Each seemed to ask, "If I propose this solution, what difficulties will I encounter and how can I resolve them?" Each sketch put forth a tentative proposal aimed at fulfilling the program requirements. When these proposals could not be evaluated sufficiently, due to a lack of knowledge, further investigation led to another series of enquiries. For example, the first floor plan (Figure 14) could not be evaluated without understanding its impact on the floor below, so the next sketch considered this (Figure 15). This illustration, in turn, raised issues about the appropriateness of bedrooms on the lowest level. So, I drew more sketches (Figures 16–20) to examine the possibility of putting all four bedrooms on the second floor. This alternative showed large areas of leftover, unprogrammed space on the ground floor—an inefficiency and added cost, along with the larger, less appropriate massing for the house, which seemed sufficiently convincing to put aside the tentative concerns about ground floor bedrooms. Thus, I attempted to work out an acceptable split bedroom scheme (Figures 21 and 22).

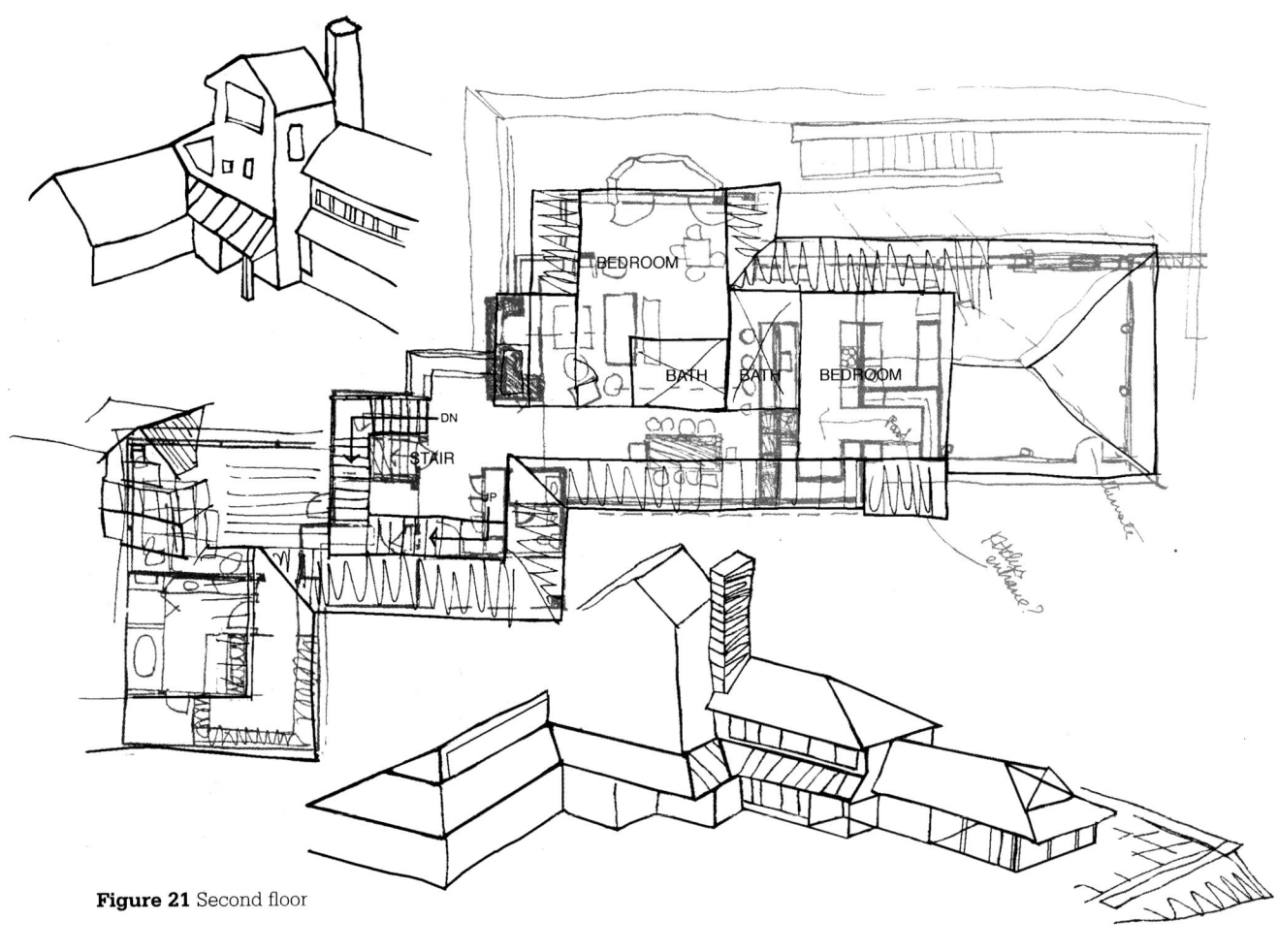

Figure 21 Second floor

Figures 21 and 22

These sketches picked up on the thinking that began in Figure 13, reconfirming the relationship between floors and developing roof shapes that were generated by having only two bedrooms on the top floor. In these sketches I questioned whether a hipped or gabled roof was more appropriate for some locations. The hip enabled more eave to be kept low, reducing the apparent scale of the house, whereas the gable admitted more light. The selection of roofing material also affects this decision. Asphalt shingle was considered as a roofing material, while wood shingle was rejected as too expensive and a fire risk for this remote location. A metal roof also seemed a valid alternative. A roof shape with fewer intersections and complications (a gabled roof) supported the idea of a simpler expression and reinforced the use of a metal roof.

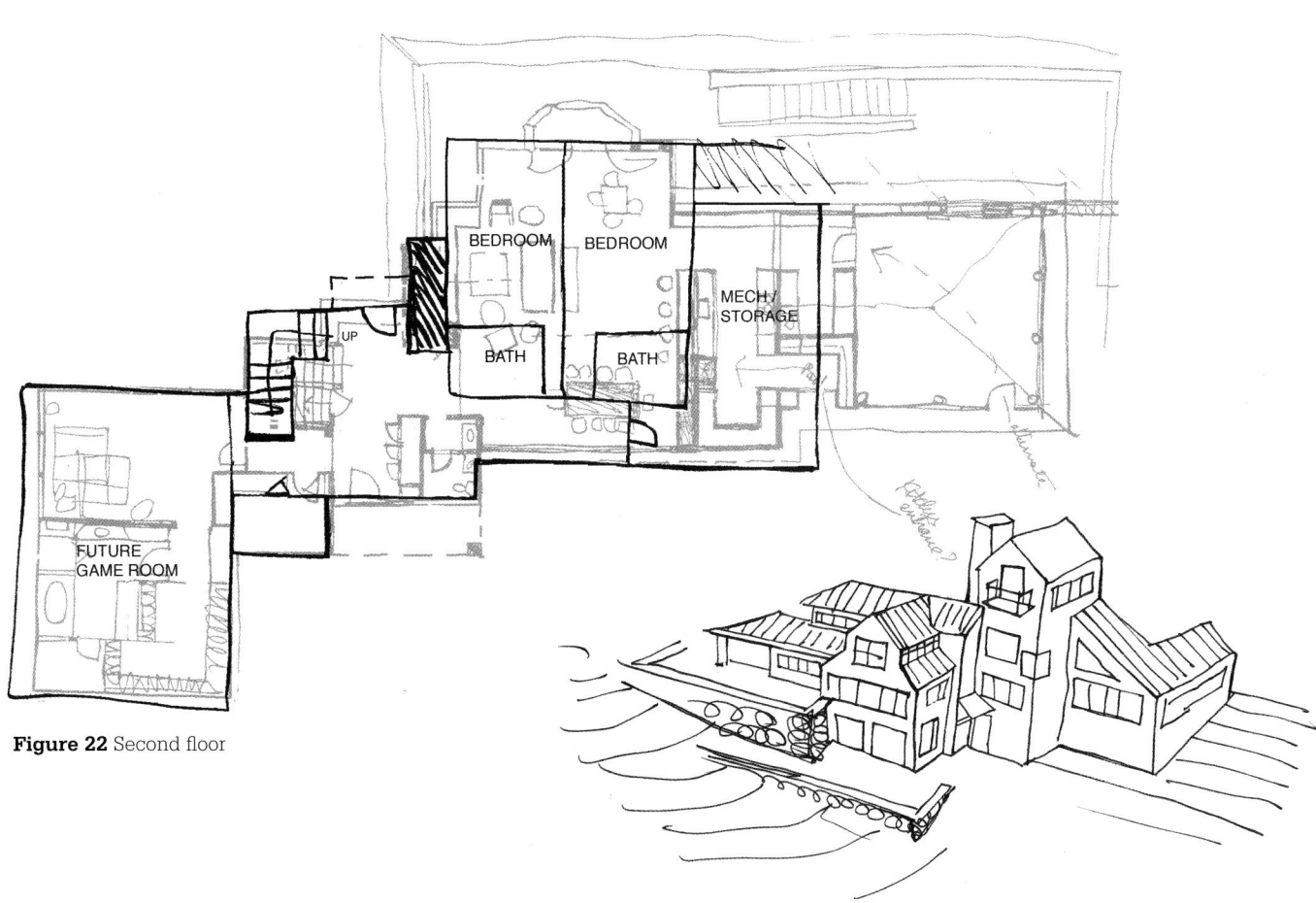

Figure 22 Second floor

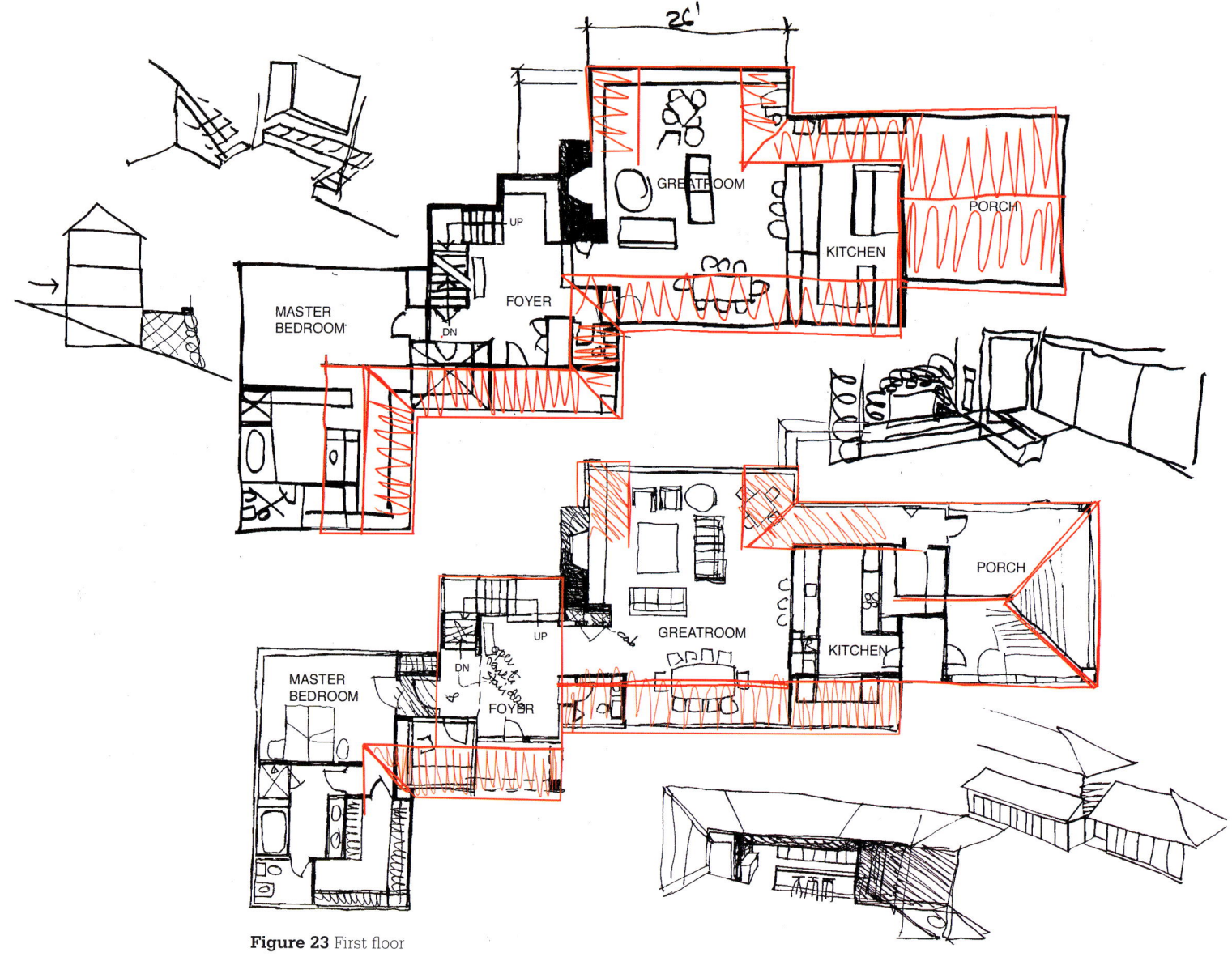

Figure 23 First floor

Figure 23

With a growing comfort that spaces were now positioned properly, I refocused attention on advancing the living areas of the house (Figures 23–26). So far, this part of the house had received only superficial attention. Now I examined it in more detail. I studied and provisionally resolved issues relating to spatial expression, the relationship to surroundings, and enclosing features. At this point, I accepted solutions as placeholders, aware that I'd make refinements and improvements later. I was creating an overall framework—an infrastructure for the house. The ongoing work of the process would be to fill in that framework with more satisfactory, fully developed spaces. These placeholder solutions enabled me to understand relationships tentatively, but I was aware that until I had examined all the affecting parameters, I could not truly evaluate a partial solution and accept it as a final design.

Figure 23 further tested how proposed roof forms would affect spaces. Would they have an adverse impact on spaces inside the house? Sloping roofs (shown in red) did impact some of the spaces. In most cases, the sloping ceilings worked well, reinforcing spatial intentions. However, in the great room there were unresolved conditions. The great room was conceived as the major living space of the house. To reflect this importance, the ceiling was tentatively set at 10 feet—high enough to feel spacious but not cavernous. In early discussions, a higher two-story space had been considered but rejected as too difficult to maintain for what was to be, primarily, a vacation retreat. Although a 10-foot ceiling meant an 11-foot climb to the second floor, keeping stair risers low could mitigate the effort, even though lower risers would translate into a longer run (more steps) for the stair.

Figure 24

Figure 24

We also had to understand the impact of the fireplace on the great room. My clients had wanted a stone fireplace with a raised hearth. This sketch laid out its design issues. Could the hearth be integrated into the space as a seat or a bench? How would such a configuration impact windows and spatial definitions? Later in the process, as the budget became more defined and flexible floor space more critical, the raised hearth, which required more floor area than a flush hearth, was deleted.

Figure 25

It was not yet clear to me how the kitchen should relate to the great room. Should it be part of the space or should each area be separate and distinct? Given the informal nature of the house, the favored solution treated the kitchen as a separate but contiguous space. Its ceiling was lowered slightly to express the separation. This delineation also helped to define a more coherent rectangular shape for the more spacious great room. The kitchen became part of the great room, but subordinate to it—a kind of adjacent alcove.

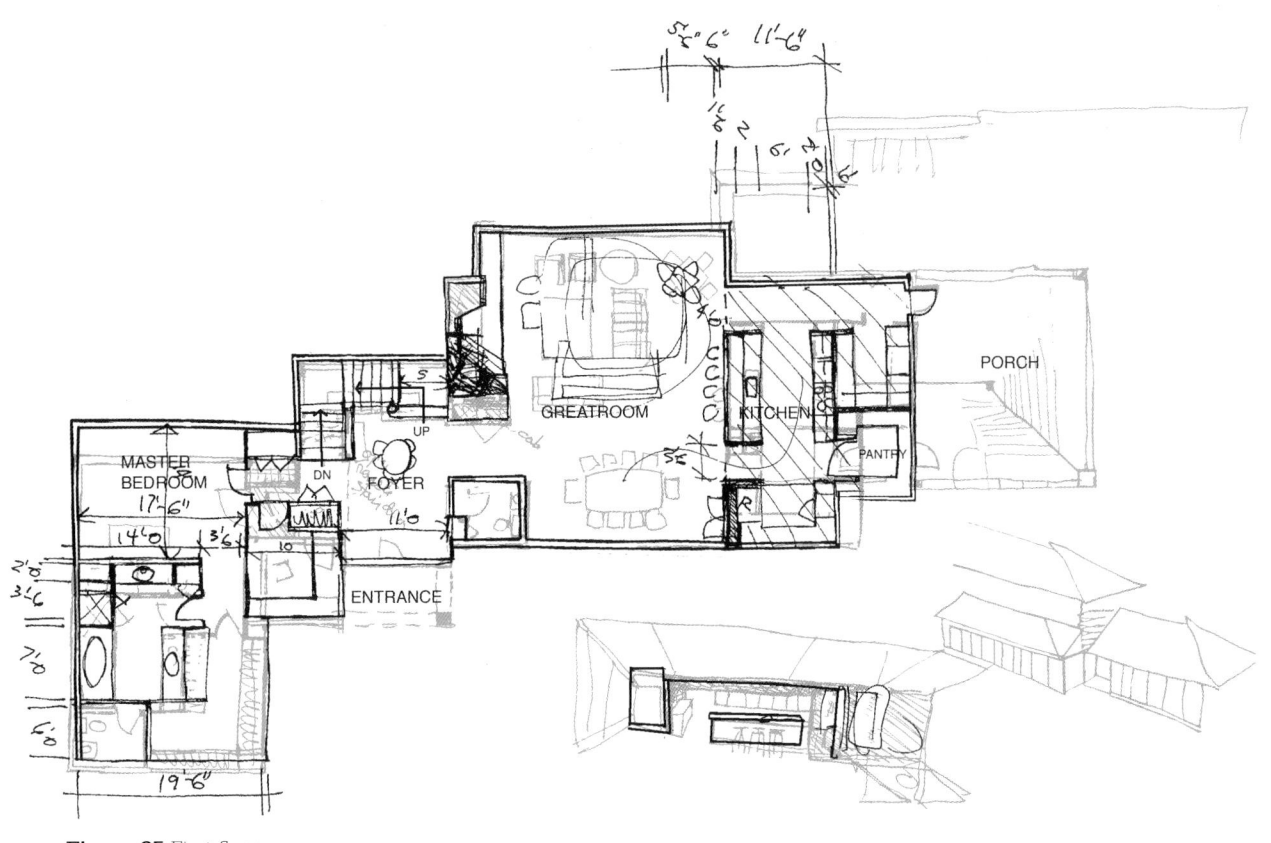

Figure 25 First floor

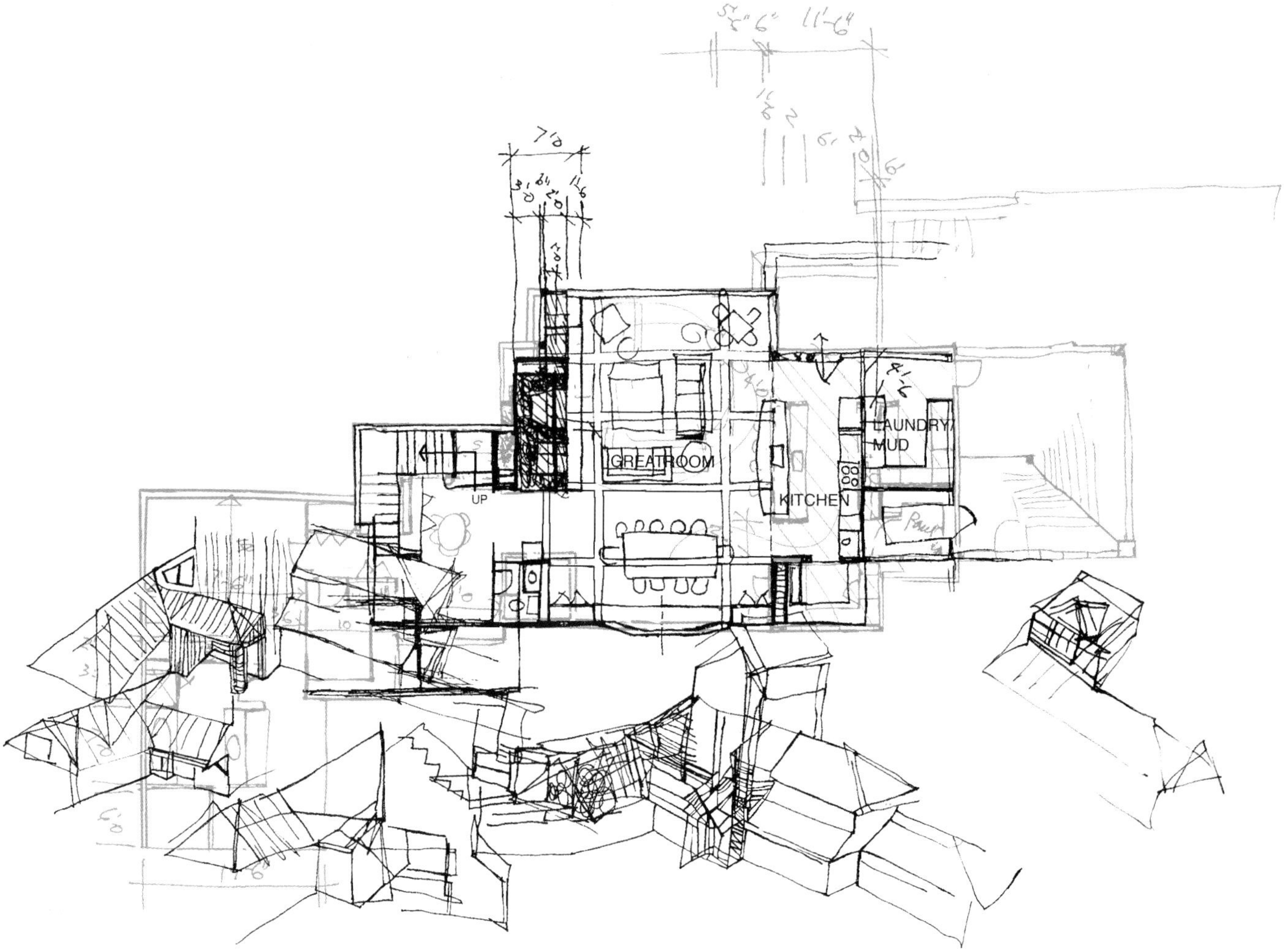

Figure 26 Second floor

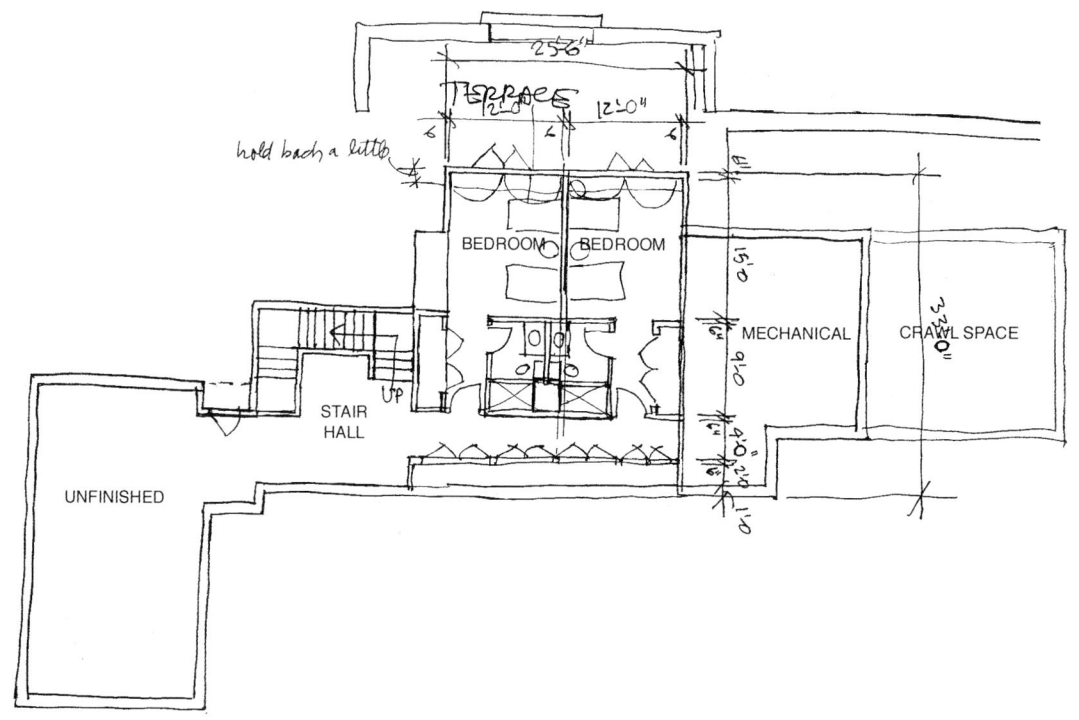

Figure 27 Ground floor

Figure 26

In this overlay, I defined the great room further by integrating the ceiling structure into a visually logical beam pattern. The structure and ceiling in a portion of the dining area needed to slope to accommodate the low eave height on the exterior of the house (see the section, Figure 29). I needed to carefully work out how the sloped portion of the ceiling would be integrated into the character of the great room.

Figures 27–29

Until now, much of the design process involved issues associated with satisfying the program and finding an overall organization for the house. I compiled my accumulated knowledge in a revised set of drawings. I had been working without drafting equipment and needed a more accurate check on my relatively loose free-hand sketches. I fixed critical dimensions, both horizontal and vertical, to prepare for more accurate computer-aided drawings that would confirm the size of the house. As I drew the plans, I once again mentally walked through the spaces:

- was the definition of the space and form clear and appropriate?
- could people move comfortably from space to space?
- would their movement be direct and unobstructed?
- was I developing vistas within the house and taking advantage of views to the surroundings?
- were spaces appropriately defined?
- was there spatial interest and variety?
- could furniture be arranged easily?
- was there flexibility in the shape of spaces to allow for variations in furniture arrangement, so that the space could adapt to changes in lifestyle?
- were window openings properly located and proportioned to accommodate views, take advantage of the sun and breezes, and control glare?
- were entrances to spaces appropriately located and proportioned to provide ease of circulation, to ensure privacy and security, to reinforce spatial connections or separations, to provide visual cues for clear orientation, and to relate properly to other architectural elements?
- would doors swing in the proper direction?
- could they be opened and remain open without conflict?
- was the structure appropriately addressed?
- did the expression of structure (columns and beams) 'fit' with the spatial intentions of the space?

The architecture of the house was responding to the unique nature of the site. The plan—the result of maximizing views and capturing southern sun—had developed logically into a long, relatively narrow shape. Running parallel to the slope, the house was set into the mountainside. Pitched roofs hinted at the snowy winter climate. The tower and large glass areas implied the exceptional views.

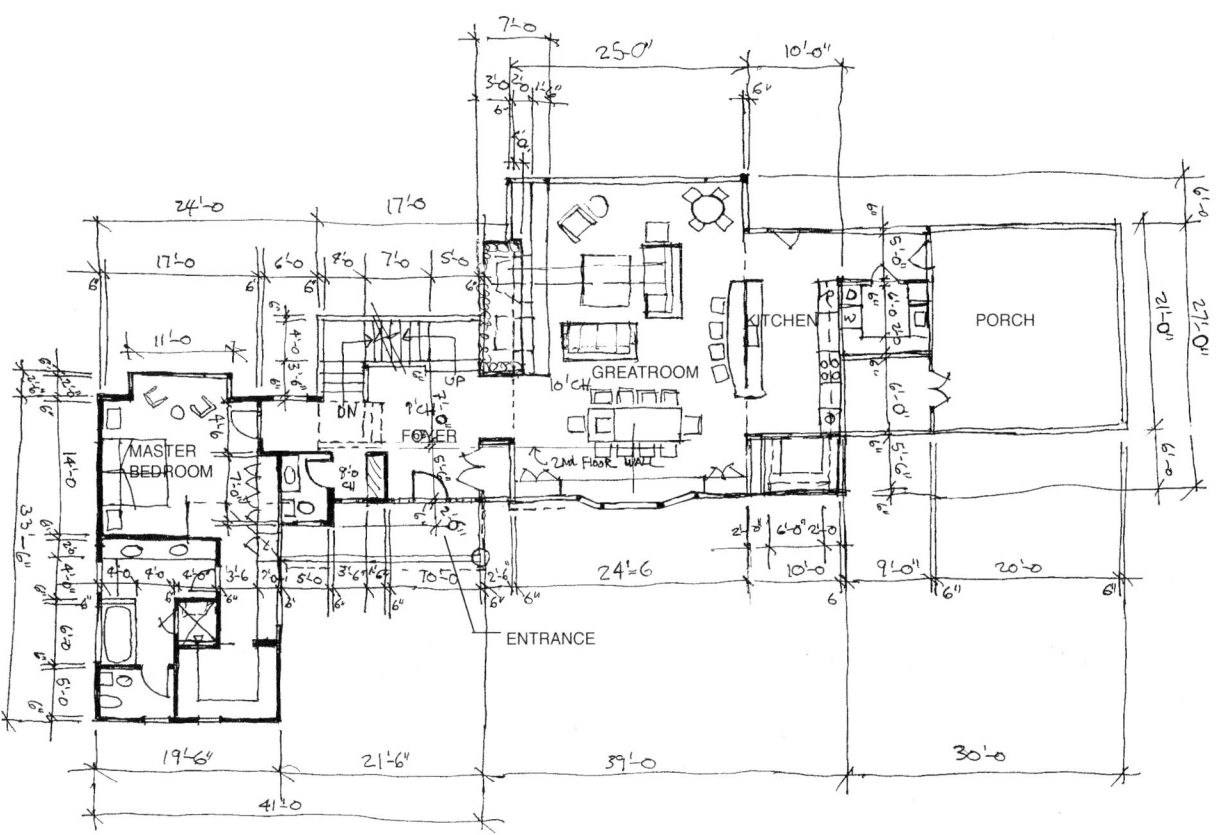

Figure 28 First floor

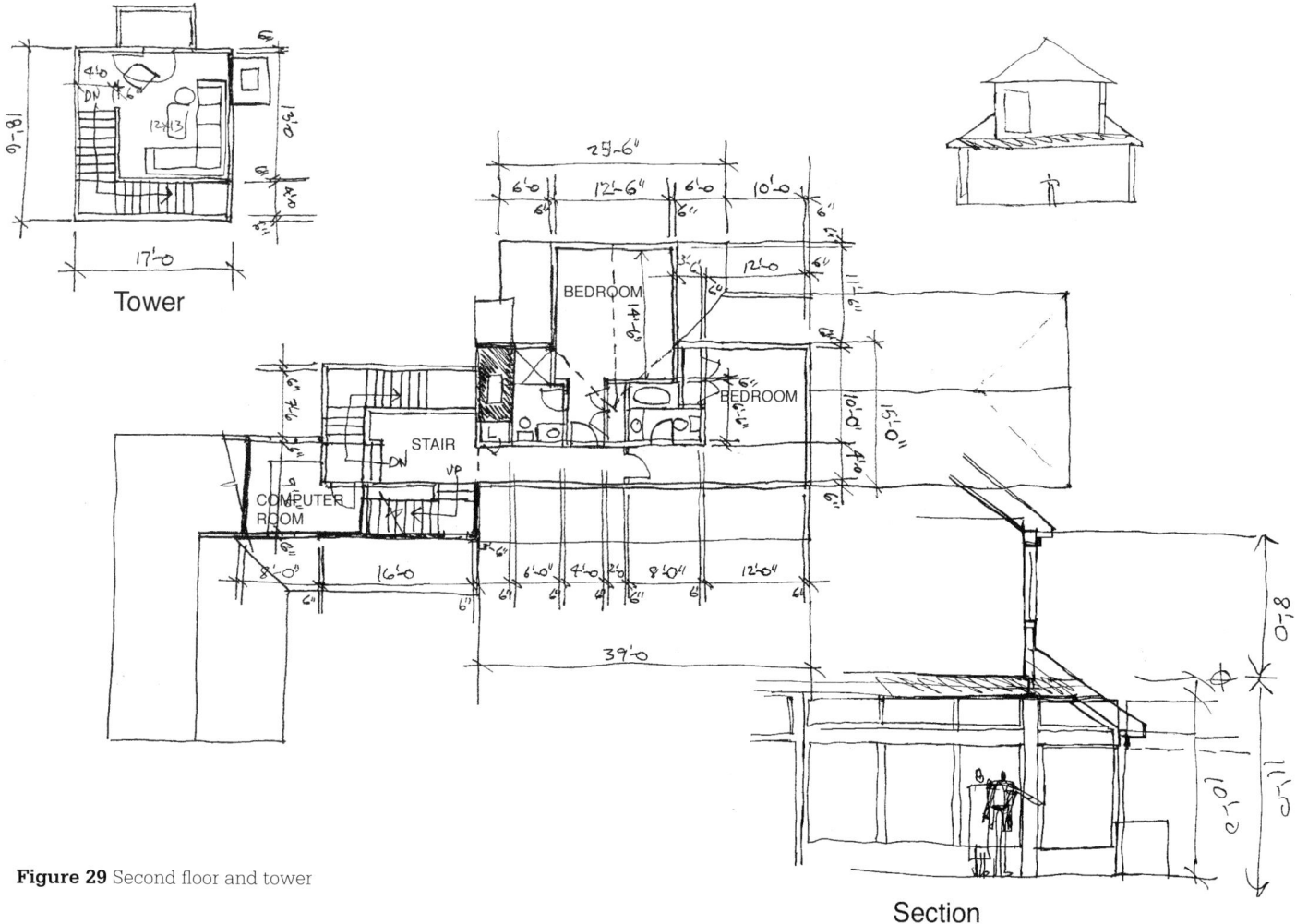

Figure 29 Second floor and tower

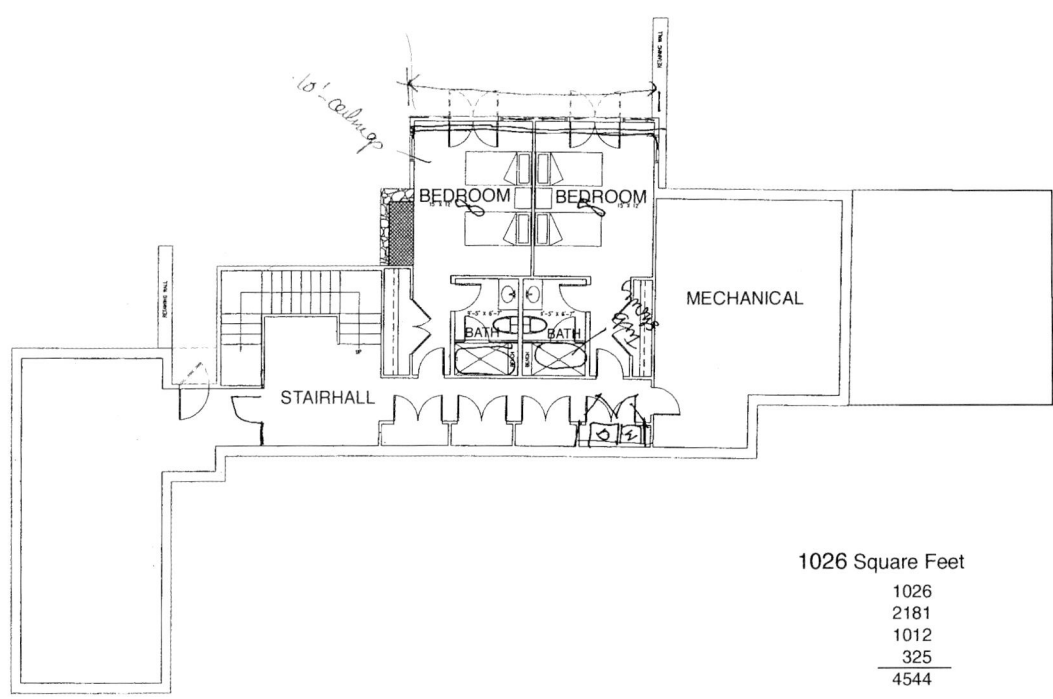

Figure 30 Ground floor

Figures 30–35

The plans were redrawn on the computer. From them, elevations and sections were laid out for use as accurate base drawings for ongoing elevation studies. Roof slopes and some tentative locations for windows and doors were inserted. Using the cost-per-square-foot-of-construction as a guide, the estimated cost of the house was recalculated and checked against the budget to ensure that the proposed scheme was 'in the budgetary ballpark'. It was still larger than desired. I proposed eliminating some space where the reduction would not be too consequential. With my clients' concurrence, I made the changes.

Now, with floor plans and space configurations functioning reasonably, I shifted my attention to refining the house's exterior shape and expression. The rural environment and the use of the house as a vacation 'cottage' had suggested simple geometric profiles for its expression. Also, keeping forms uncomplicated would help minimize construction hurdles and make waterproofing more direct and reliable. I built up and combined basic geometric shapes to create an overall architectural image. Expressing smaller component elements visually reduced the overall mass and helped create an appropriately scaled residential expression. The articulation of the mass also suggested local indigenous architecture—a natural outgrowth of this climate and place. The indigenous architecture possessed an informality, which enlivened its appearance. I hoped to capture that same spontaneity in this house.

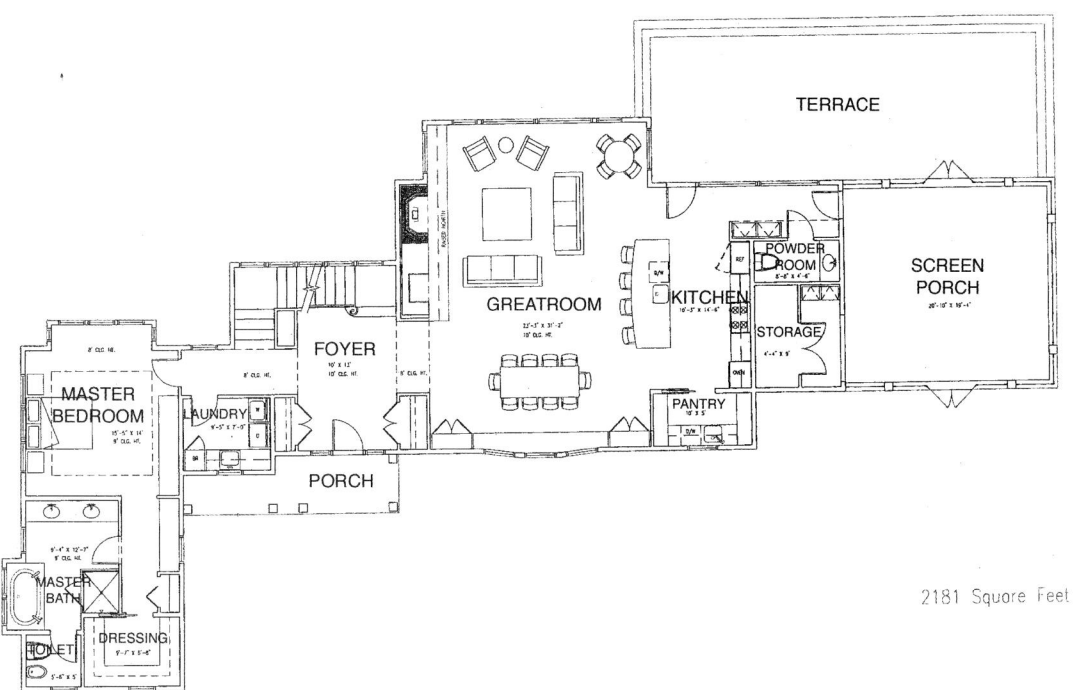

Figure 31 First floor

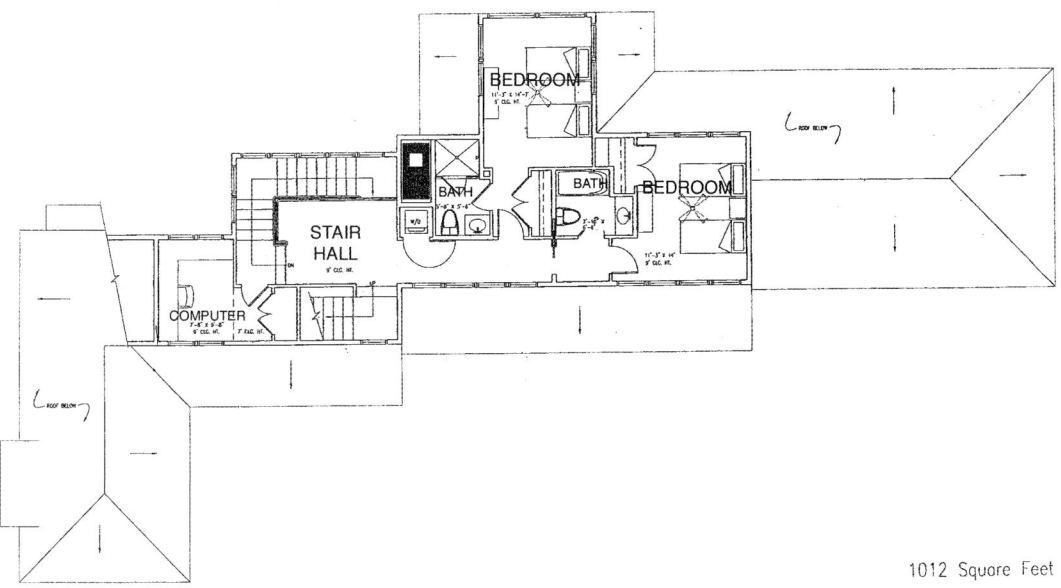

Figure 32 Second floor

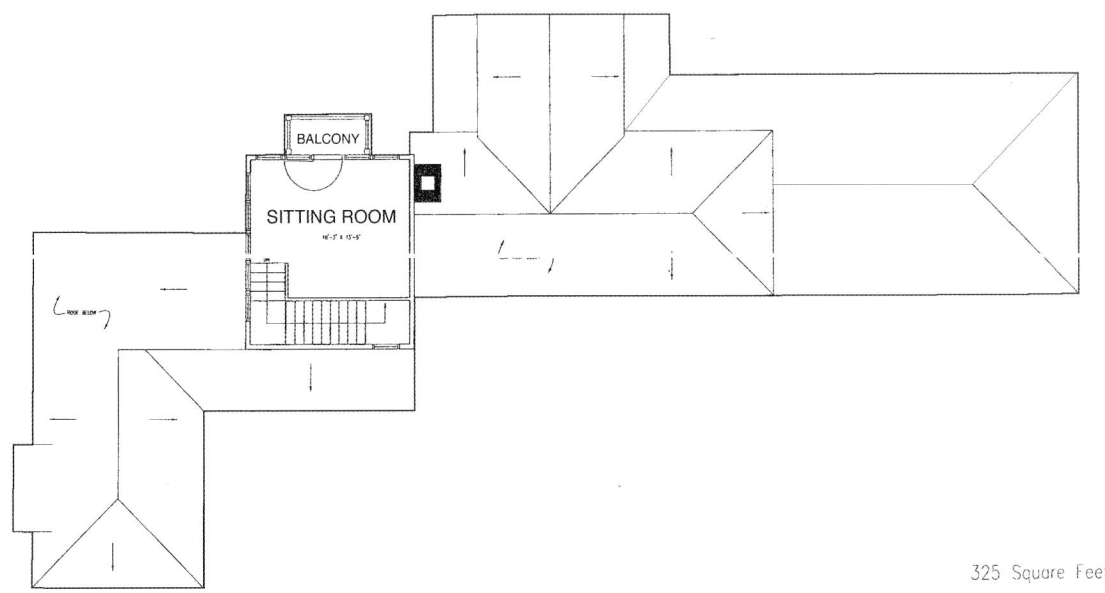

Figure 33 Tower and roof

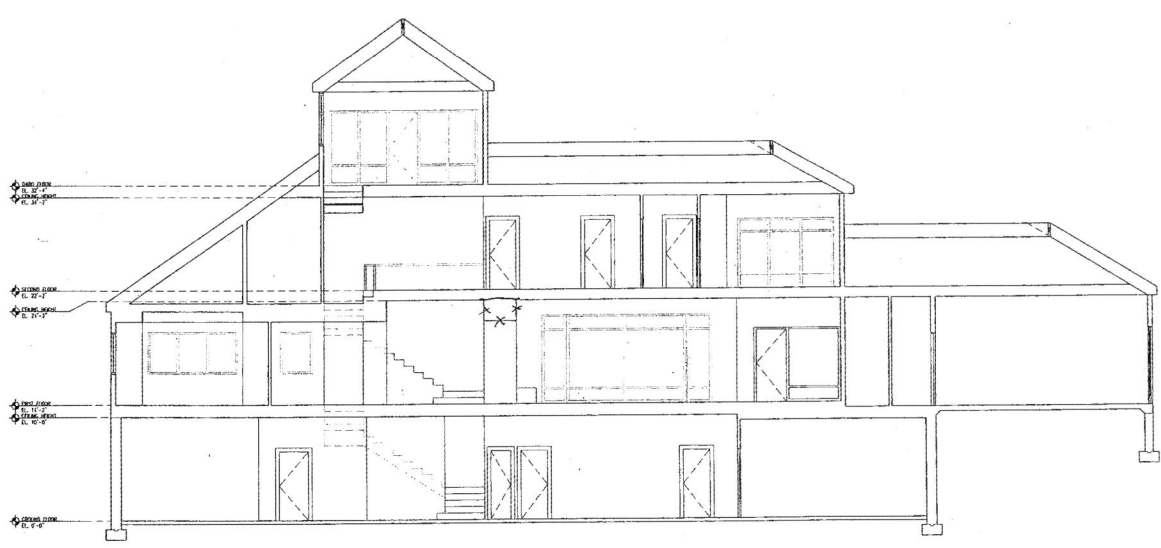

Figure 34 Building section

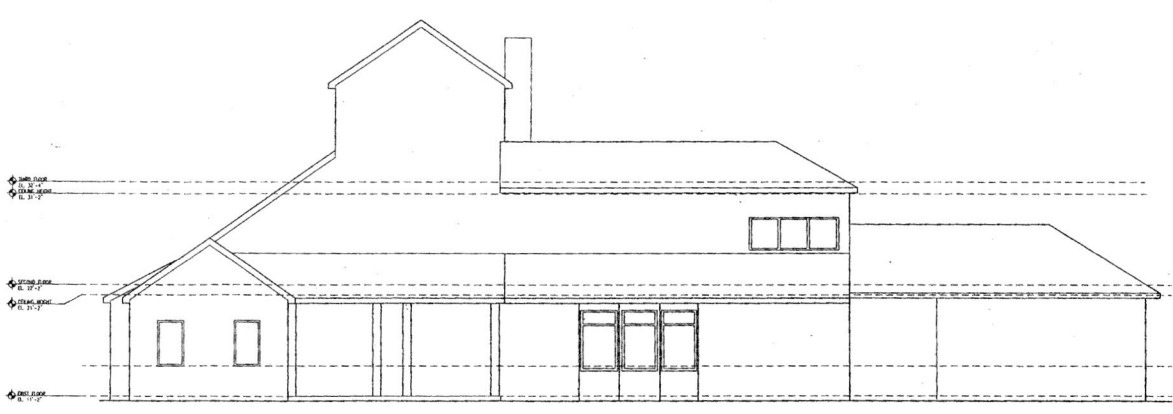
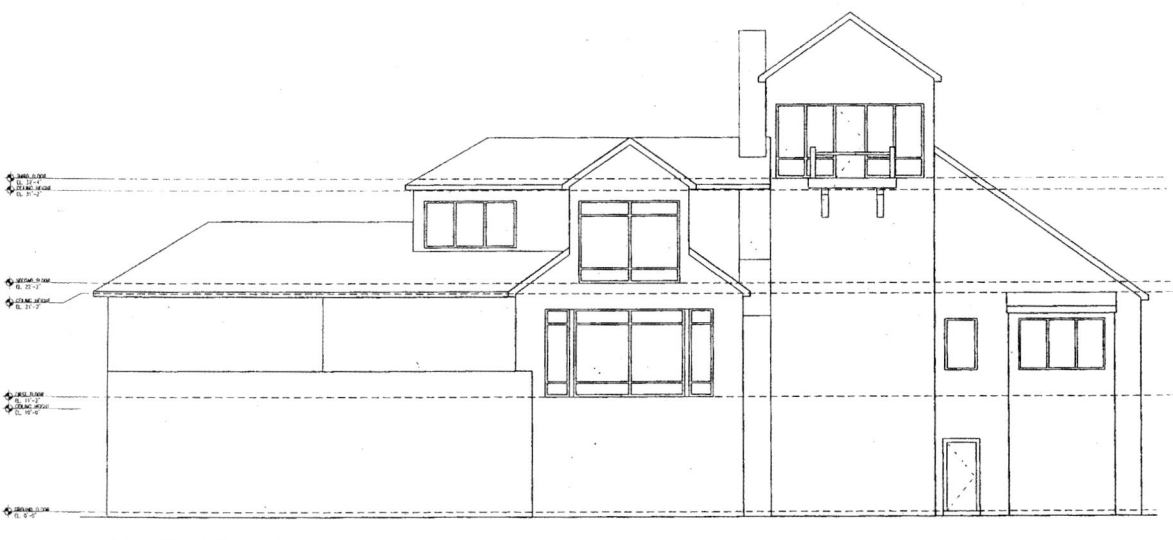

Figure 35 South elevation (top);
North elevation (bottom)

Figure 36

Glass size, proportions, the relationship of one element to another and the degree of solid to void all affected the composition of the façade. Previous studies had highlighted plan changes that would facilitate a more integrated form expression. Where appropriate, I adjusted the plans to incorporate the modifications. Elevation studies were drawn to further test relationships. Window sizes and locations needed to satisfy interior requirements, as well as compositional concerns on the exterior. This elevation facing the long view suggested lots of glass, but the size of windows and their location had to be appropriate to the spaces and activities taking place within. I also continued to work on the massing of the house. I wanted building elements, especially roofs, to connect to one another logically, intersections and transitions to be built simply, and the form of the house to appear direct and uncomplicated. I was trying to create a unified composition with sufficient variety to provide interest.

I explored cladding materials, including vertical board siding, which is expressive of the rural architecture. Later, I rejected vertical board siding and vertical board and batten siding as too narrow for the long wall surfaces. Wider boards, which would be more in scale, would have been dimensionally unstable. To lower construction costs, I wanted to use building materials that were relatively easy to procure in this rural location. I also considered in detail the building's relationship to adjacent grades. In this sketch I explored stone for the base of the house. It visually reinforced the idea that the house was anchored to the ground and engaged with the mountainside but, unfortunately, its relatively high cost made me wary of its use.

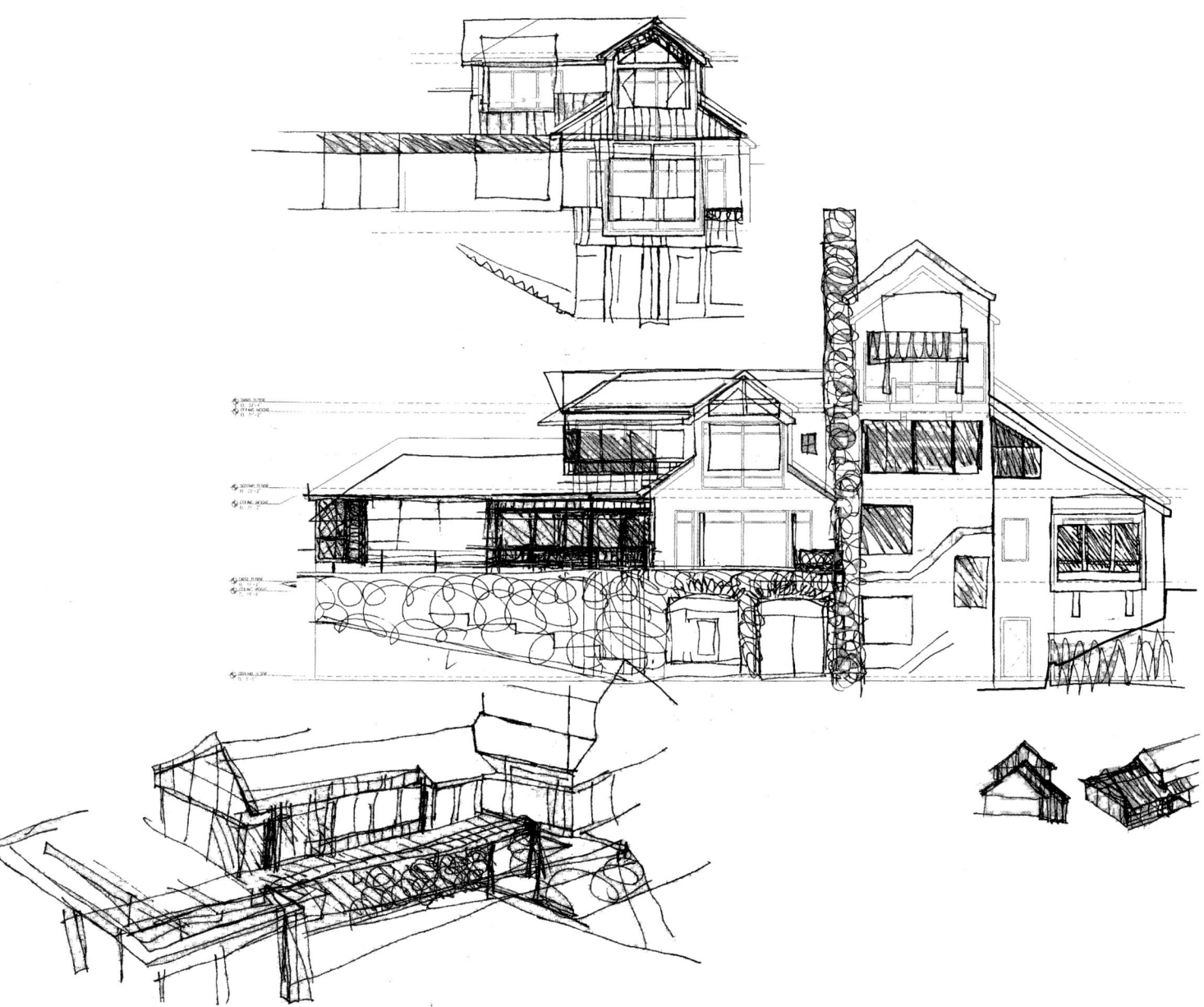

Figure 36

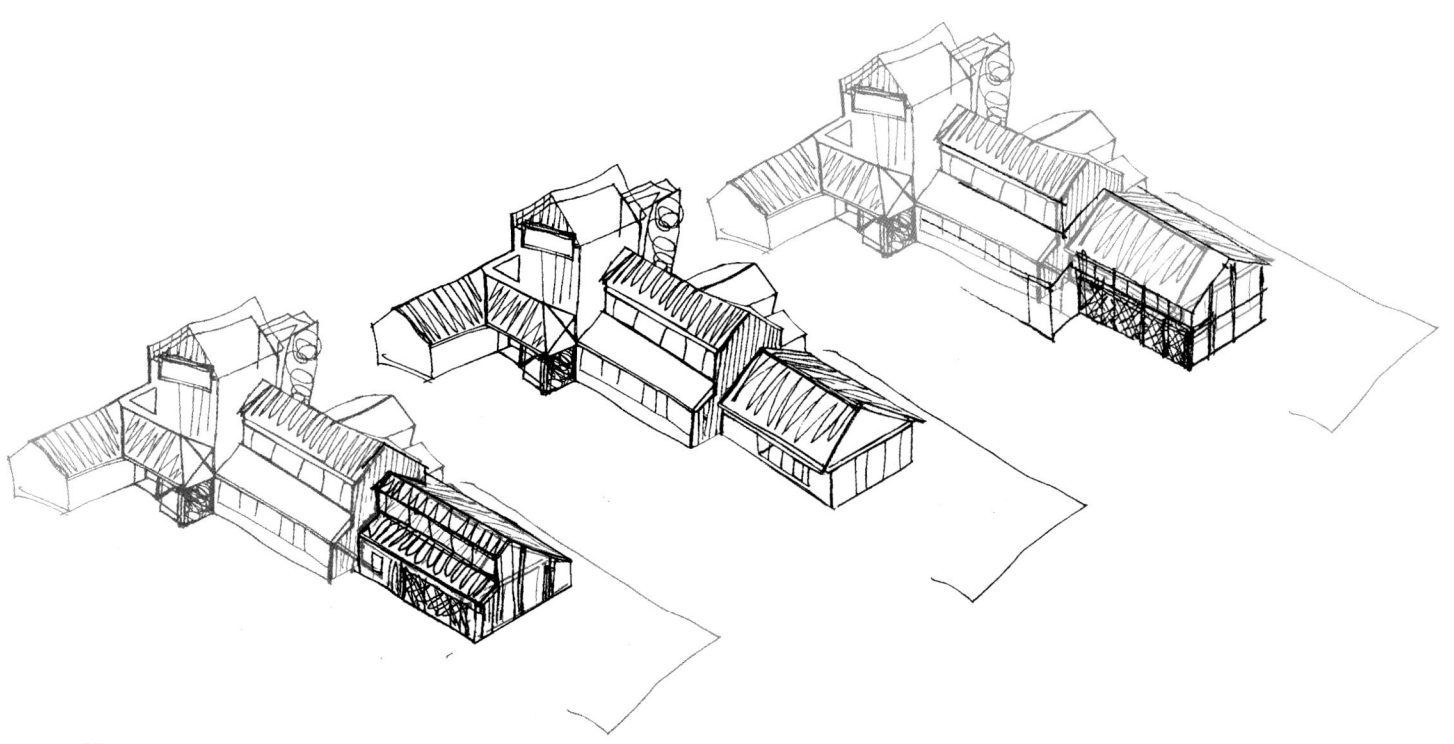

Figure 37

Figure 37
To give the house a more intimate scale, I broke up its mass into smaller sections. I kept the higher two-story elements central, buffering them with lower one-story sections along the periphery. This segmentation helped reduce the scale of the house, but it still required better transitions between components so that they would appear more integrated. As I worked, I was continually trying to compositionally balance visual clarity and simplicity with the variegated and unexpected. For me, order without variety is boring, but variety without order is chaos.

Figure 38

A sketch of the house from the downhill (northern) side detailed my further study of transitional issues. I explored the option of having a projecting deck adjacent to the great room. The complications caused by my initial desire to have nothing interrupting the panoramic view from the great room had limited easy movement from indoors to outside. This option allowed outdoor living directly accessible from the great room.

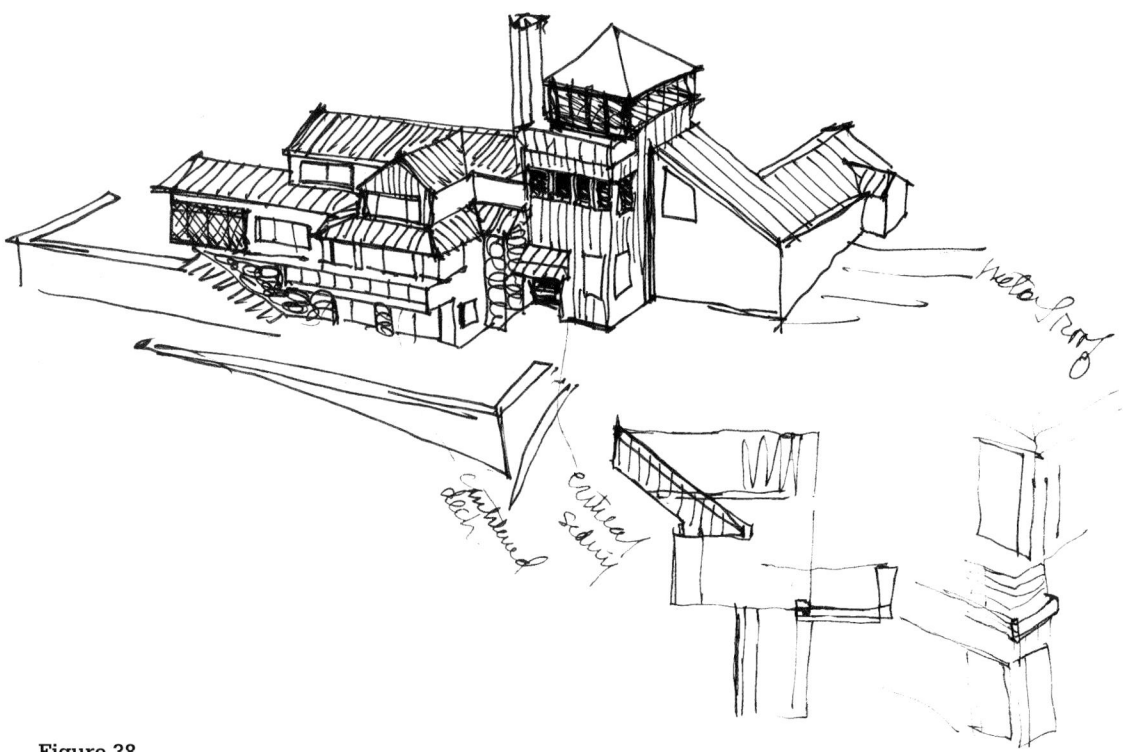

Figure 38

Figure 39

These sketches focused on the deck and tower. They examined the concern of the quality of the lower bedrooms. Would the projecting deck compromise daylight to the bedrooms? In the final design, tall 11-foot-high ceilings and large wrap-a-round windows helped mitigate the loss of light. I also wrestled with how to shape and structure the deck and how to design its underside to create a pleasing expression looking out from the lower-level bedrooms. These sketches also tentatively explored extending the stone base onto the tower.

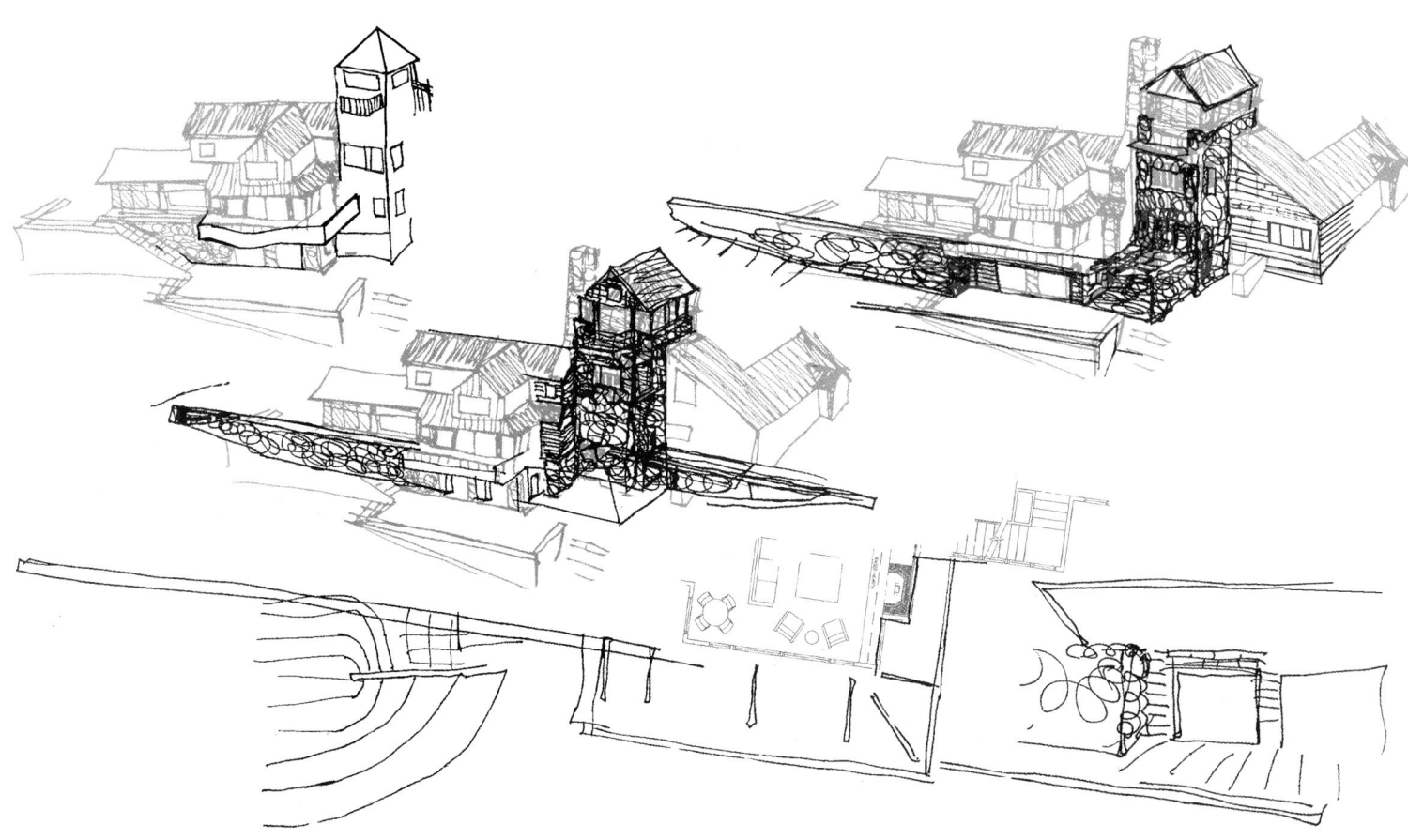

Figure 39

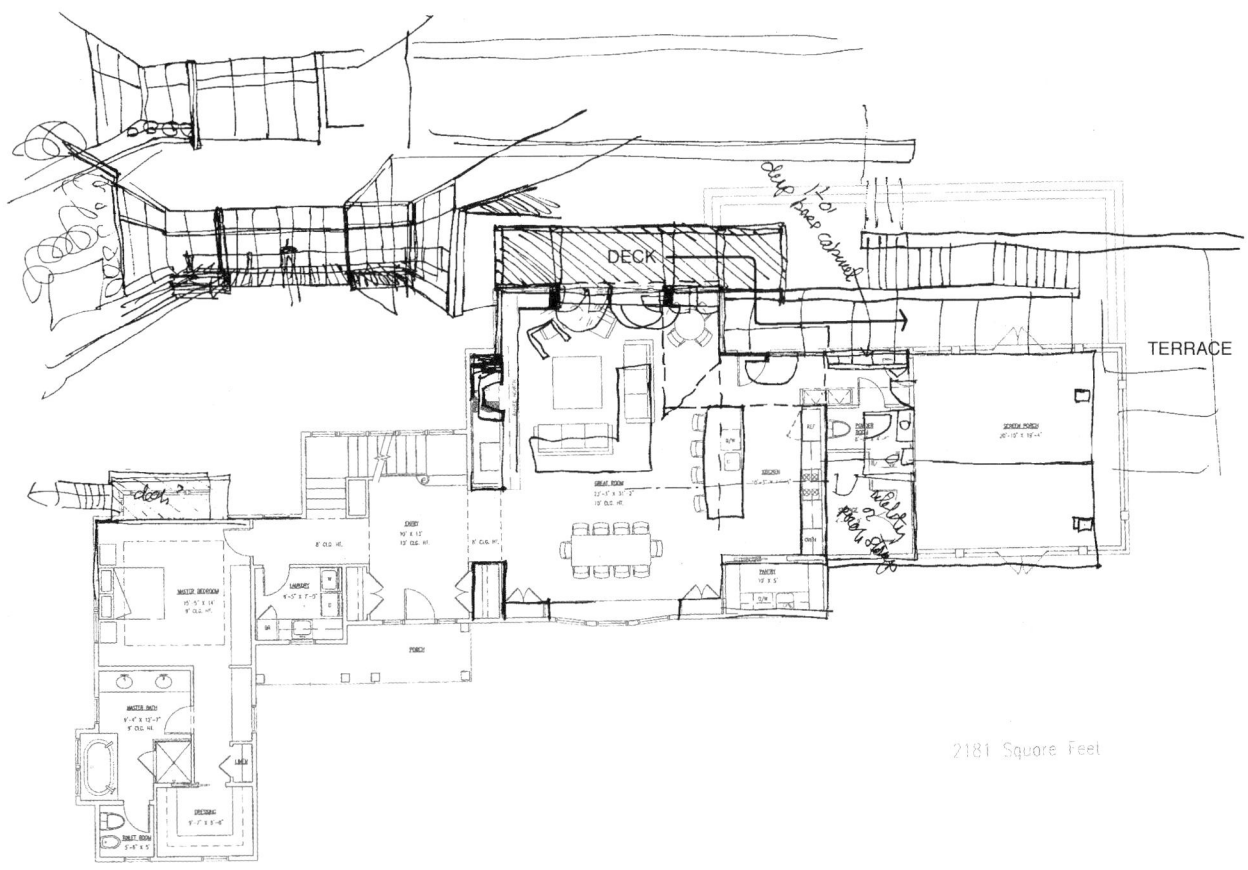

Figure 40 First floor

Figure 40

In this sketch, I examined how the deck would function and affect views from the great room. The deck, shown here, was initially considered a small cantilevered walkway, primarily intended as a path leading to the southern-oriented terrace.

Figure 41

Here, I drew a larger, more usable deck that wraps around the great room with columns for support.

Figure 41

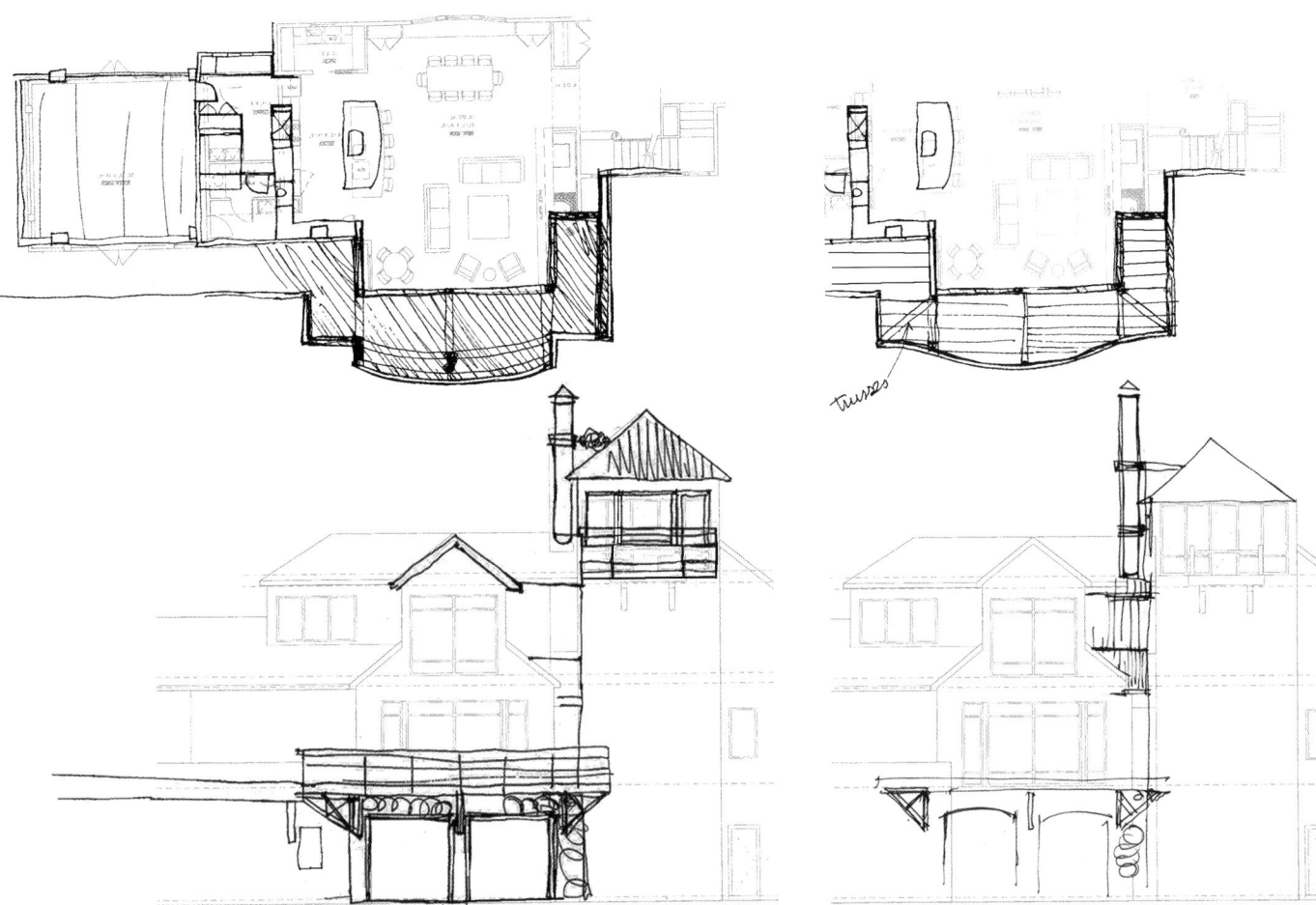

Figure 42

Figure 42
Supporting the deck on posts would infringe on views from the bedrooms below. These sketches proposed supporting it with wall brackets instead.

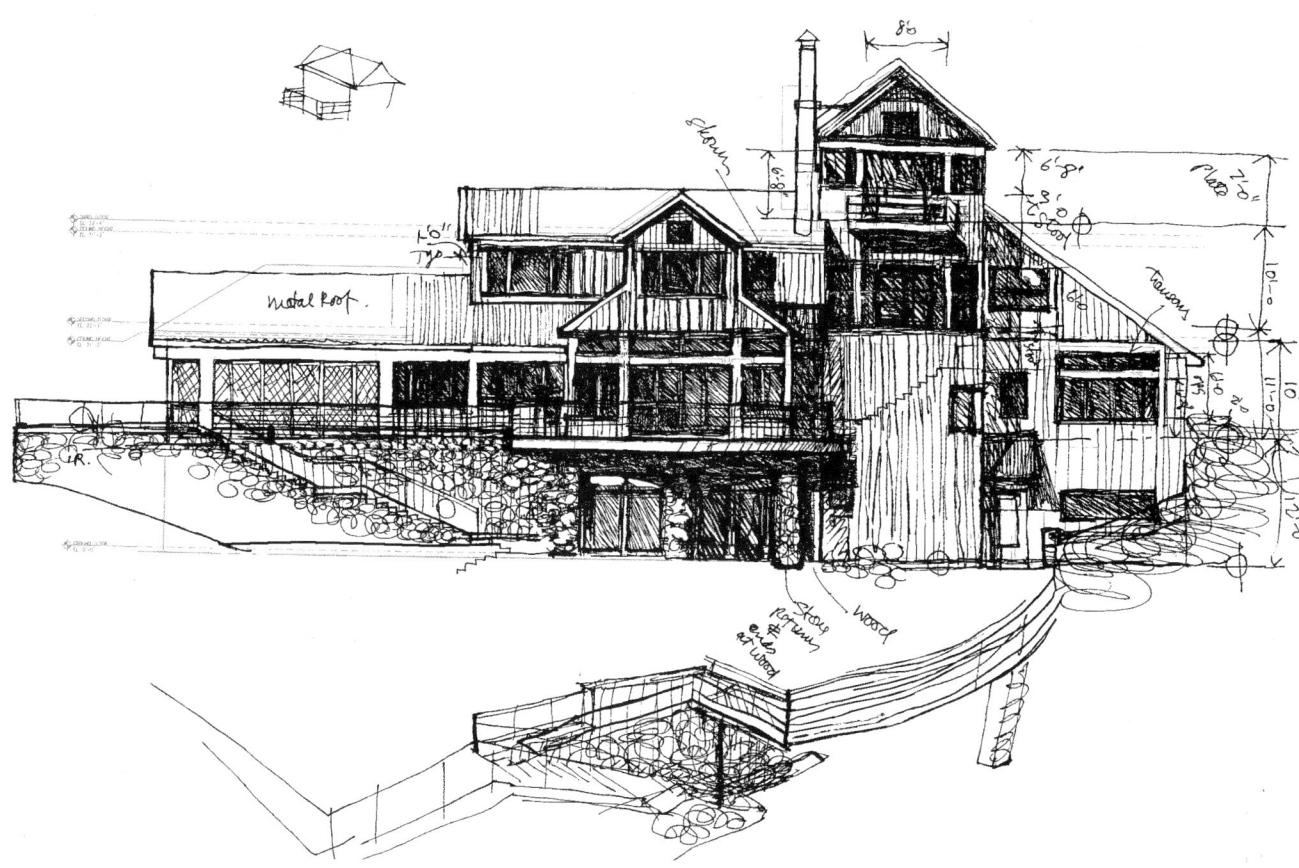

Figure 43 North elevation

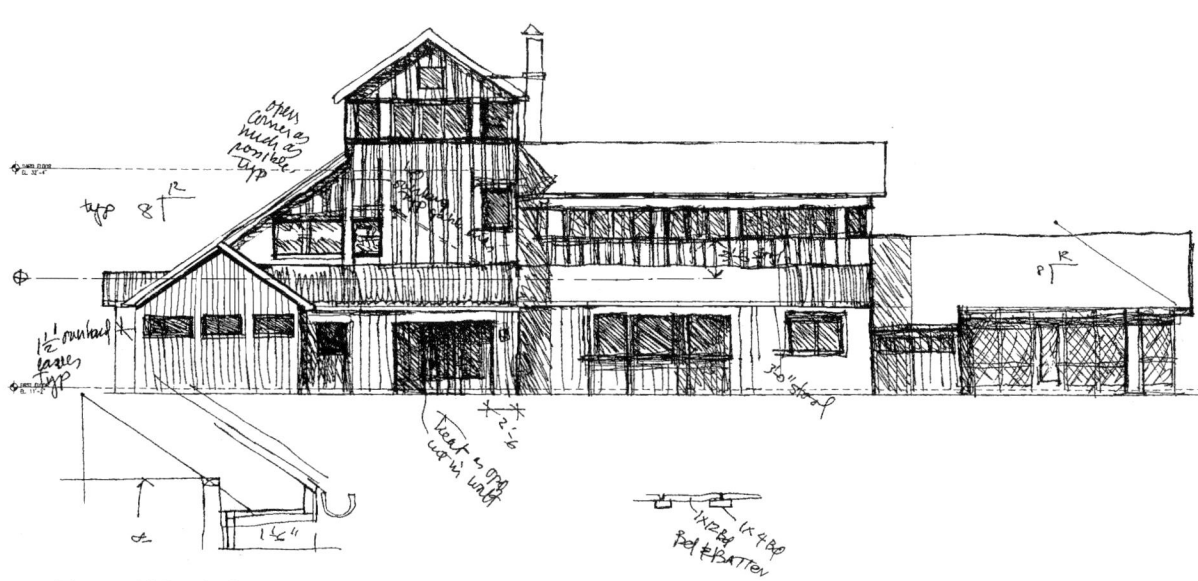

Figure 44 South elevation

Figure 43

This elevation consolidates the results of previous studies. I refined the height and slope of roofs, fenestration and the relationship to grade. I drew the projecting great room deck cantilevered and supported by one stone pier. The chimney is shown as metal rather than stone complimented by a metal roof and vertical board siding. I verified the height of the structure so that floor-to-floor dimensions and the angle of roof slopes ensured the house met legal height limits.

Figure 44

A similar composite elevation from the south reconsidered the use of board and batten siding.

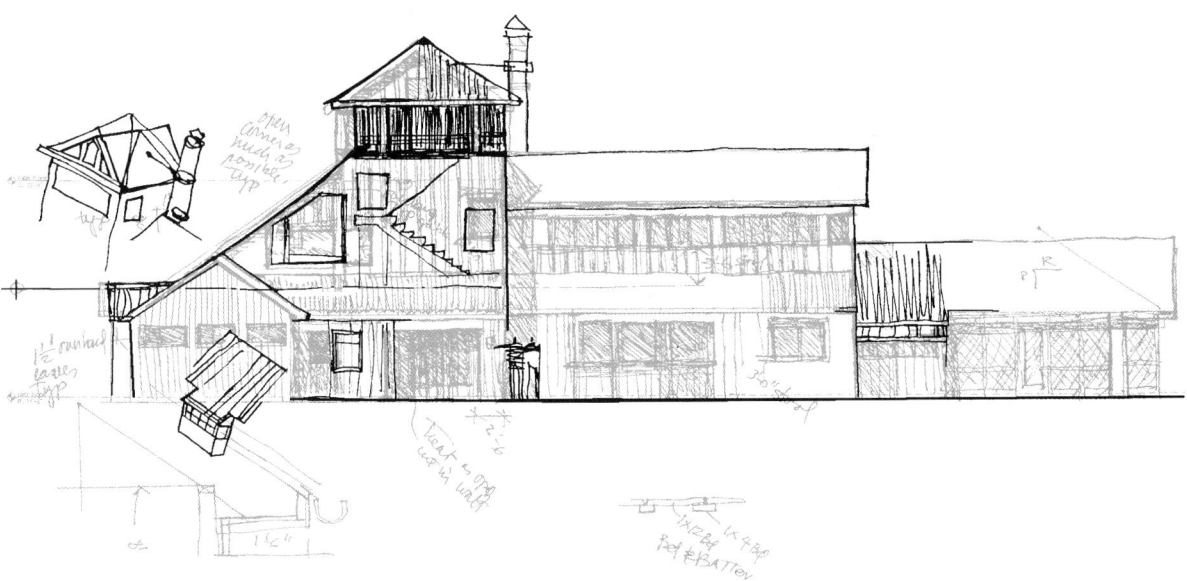

Figure 45 North elevation

Figure 45

I was uncertain about the form of the tower roof. Should the tower proclaim its centrality with a hipped roof, or should the roof be gabled, facing out to the countryside to emphasize the dominant view? An advantage of the hip was that its continuous eave suggested a lower building height. But the gabled solution seemed visually more appealing because it reinforced the direction of the panoramic view, opened the space to more light, and gave the opportunity for a more interesting and voluminous ceiling configuration. I also examined other window options to resolve interior accommodation with exterior appearance. I studied options for minor roof extensions as well, to find forms compatible with metal roof applications.

Figure 46

With fenestration more resolved, I once again reconsidered exterior siding options. Vertical board siding still seemed too delicate for the house's expansive wall surfaces. The high walls would require an intermediate horizontal joint that would disrupt the wall's vertical continuity. Shingles offered a solution. A larger, less delicate scale could be achieved by expanding the height of each course.

Figure 46 South elevations

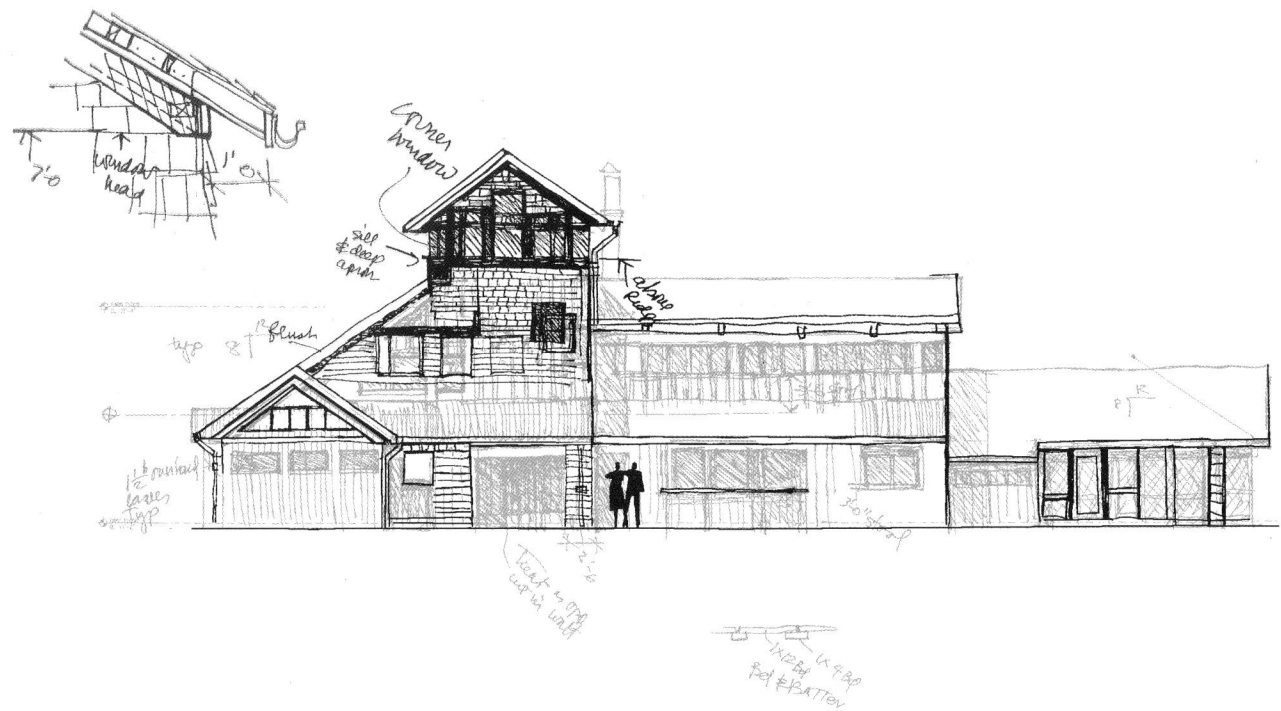

Figure 47 South elevation

Figure 47

Drawing at a small scale has the advantage of perceiving an entire composition at one time but can make it difficult to comprehend the size something will appear once built. What seems proportionally correct in a drawing may not be when built. In these elevation sketches, I used scale figures to help me comprehend and evaluate dimensional relationships. The size and proportion of windows and doors, their relative position, trim dimensions, eave heights and roof overhangs all need to relate to the dimensions of a person. Human scale is a critical quality in good architecture, especially in residential design. Enlarging a detail, giving it dimensions and considering the appropriateness of those dimensions at full scale was critical.

Figure 48

To become more confident with my decisions about the home's appearance, I needed to be sure that the elevations I sketched were accurate. Graphic indications of floors and ceilings were required so I could locate and properly position door and window openings. I also needed to better understand—and include in my illustrations—construction details. For this rural location, wood framing seemed to be an appropriate construction method for building the house. It was familiar, available to local builders and the most cost-effective approach given the budget.

This sketch evaluated a specific plate height—an important condition in wood frame construction. The plate height also influences the composition of exterior elevations and, in fact, the scale and massing of the entire house. This plate height was positioned to the level at which the sloping roof joists would penetrate the exterior wall. The height affected many relationships. Besides ceiling heights, it substantially determined the location of eaves and influenced the roof pitch. It also impacted window and door heights and the proportion of 'solid' wall and window 'voids'.

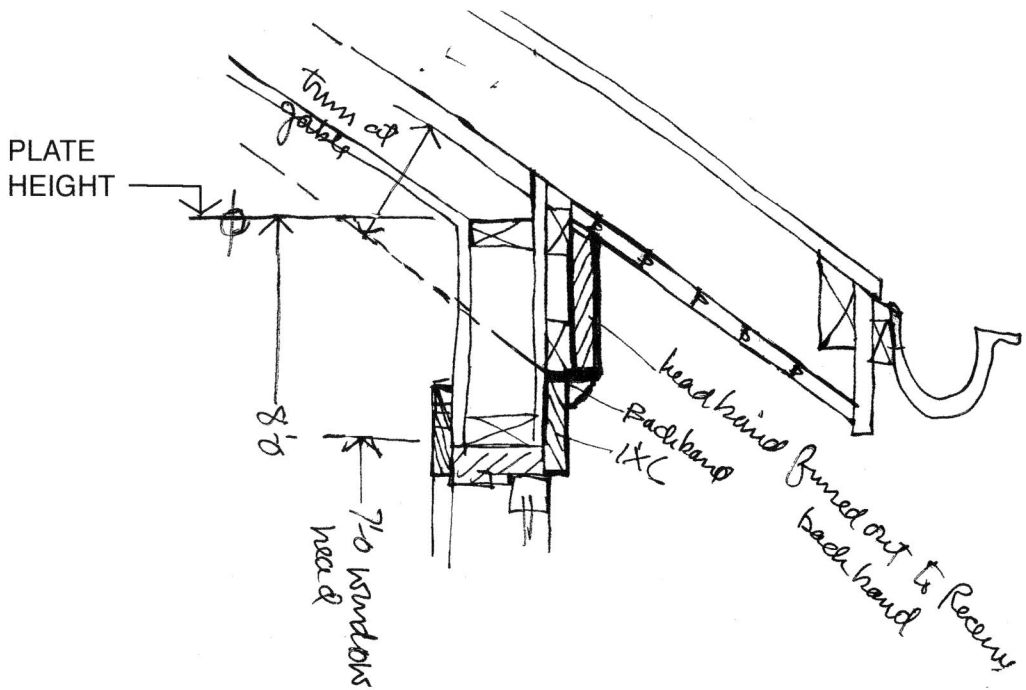

Figure 48

This sketch also explored the impact of other elements. What was an appropriate shape and expression for the roof eave? How thick should this edge appear? How far should the roof project? What should be the condition where eave meets gable and how should that intersection be expressed? What is the relationship between window trim and roof soffit? I was looking for a unifying visual consistency, a 'gestalt' to realize and refine the details of the house. I wanted the result of each new decision to fit and reinforce the larger organizing concept.

I find, as I work, that my imagination generates visual images that appear to be viable solutions to problems I am trying to solve. Sometimes, I can transform these images into workable products but there are times when it seems impossible to realize such a fit. At those times, after trying many ways to achieve results, with little or no success and with much frustration, I either give up and discard the idea or have what I call a 'creative leap' ("Eureka!"). I believe my failed attempts at reaching a satisfactory solution are the process by which we mentally achieve a thorough understanding of the relationship between all variables. Unable to find a solution where a detail fits the larger conception, we alter the larger conception to be able to accommodate the detail. A new perspective emerges and the conception is reorganized. A successful solution to the detail is now incorporated into a newly discovered and redefined context. A new solution emerges and a new vision is created, integrating all the issues successfully. This reconception is a gratifying moment in the process. For me, there is a sense of elation and relief as I discover a fresh way of viewing the problem and find a new comprehensive solution. As Le Corbusier said, "Design is a patient search."

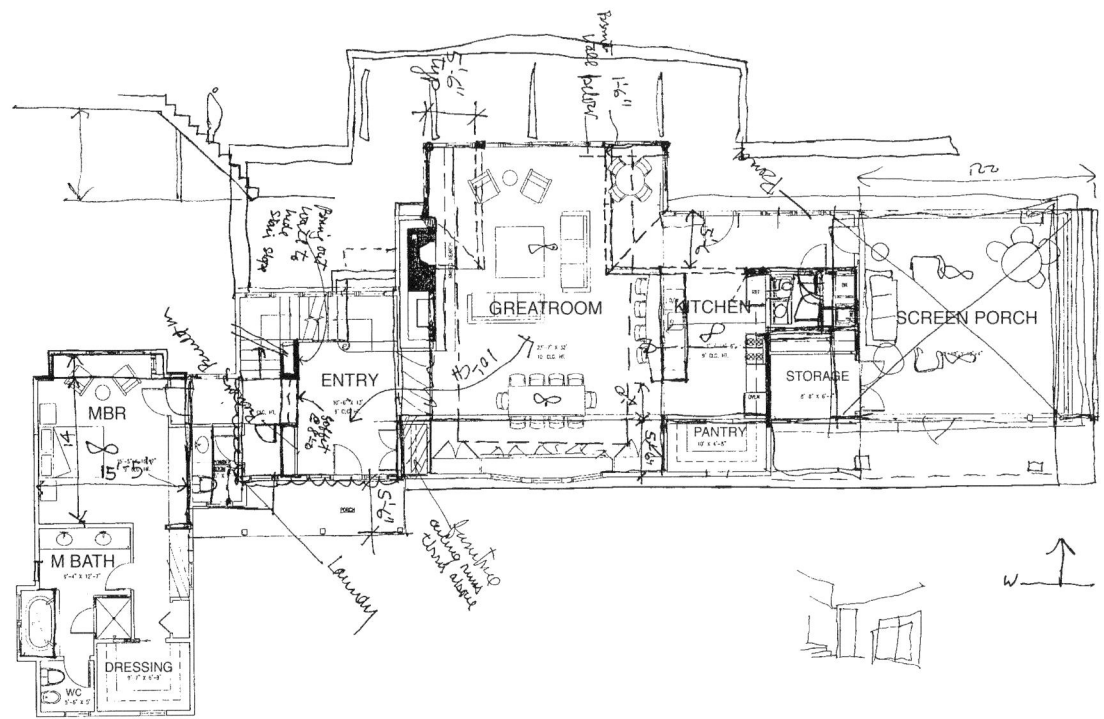

Figure 49 First floor

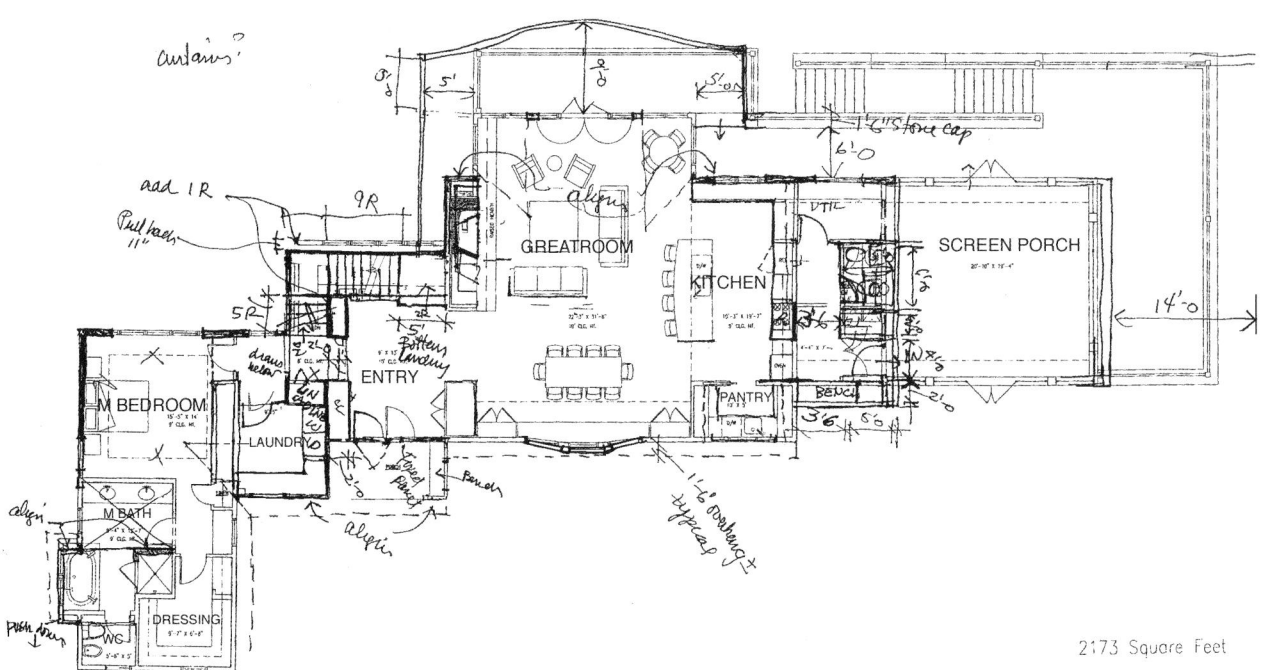

Figure 50 First floor

Figures 49–52

The focus now shifted back to finalizing a series of unresolved conditions. A major question remained as to the size, shape and structure of the deck. These sketches reexamined various forms, but a simple rectangular shape seemed, finally, most straightforward. The deck would be a wrap-around porch providing easy access from within and flexible space for outdoor living. It would be cantilevered, projecting from the core of the house, and free of the ground so as to minimally impact the ground floor bedrooms. I again reviewed each space in detail, making refinements to ensure a better fit. I reconsidered ceiling planes, definitively setting ceiling heights and dropping soffits, adjusting partition locations, affirming spatial configurations and recalculating critical dimensions. Sketches helped to inform decisions.

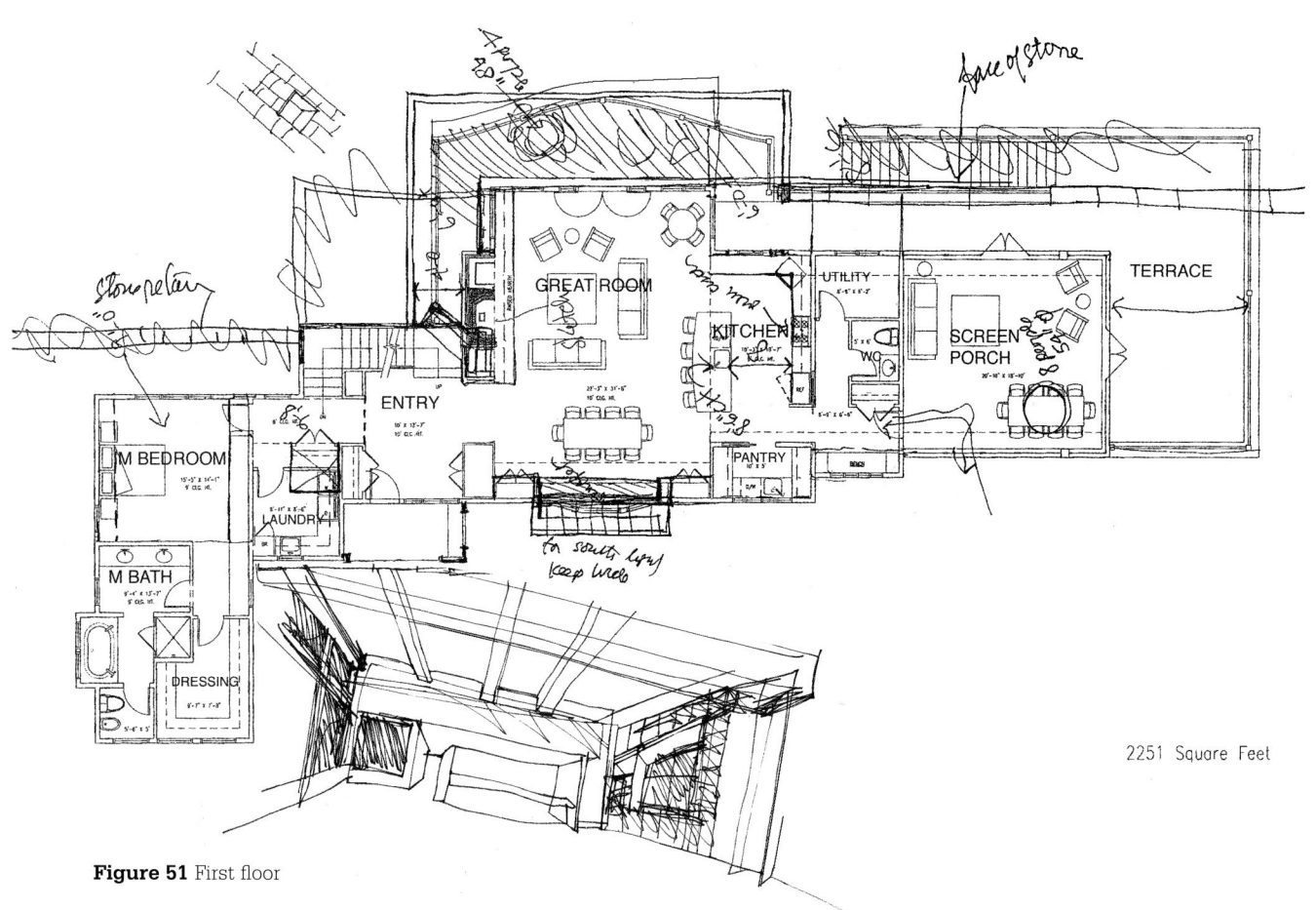

Figure 51 First floor

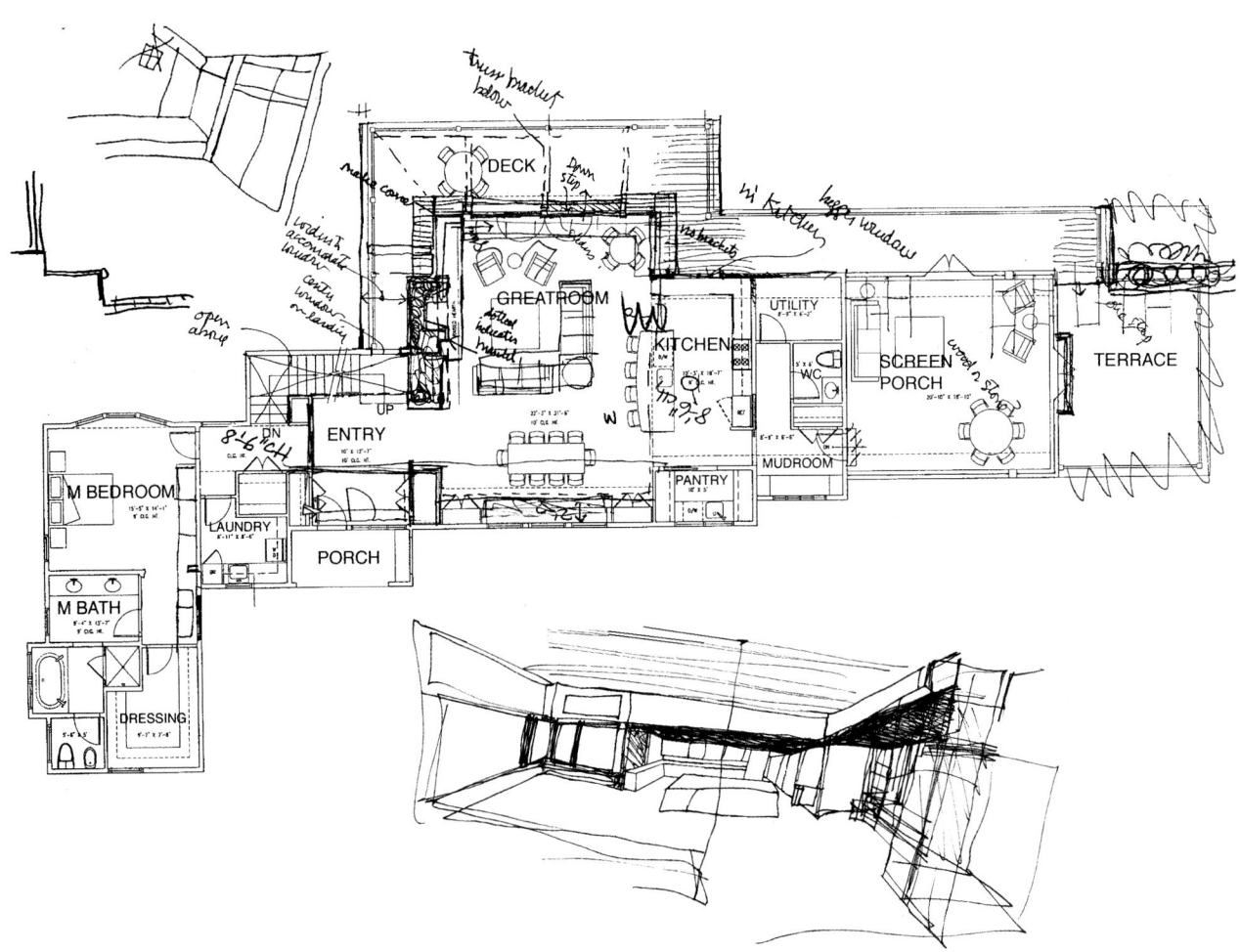

Figure 52 First floor

Figure 53

I revisited the fireplace and its relationship to the surrounding space. What would be its impact on the great room? How informal or refined should it appear? How large? What materials? Would a TV need to be integrated with it? How should stone returns be resolved? I continued to refine the fireplace design even through the construction process. The specific selection of stone, its size, scale, texture and color, and the pattern used in laying it were important considerations. But these decisions could be put off until the surrounding space was under construction so that they could be more easily understood.

Figure 53

Figure 54

Refinements were made to the second floor to respond to changes on the first floor. I modified stair treads and risers, and carefully adjusted the roof over the ground floor to fit the ceiling configuration that I was trying to achieve below. I calculated dimensions to fix critical relationships.

Figure 55

Similar refinements were made, along with cost-saving edits, to the ground floor in response to the changes occurring above. Reflected ceiling plans (drawn as if one were looking up at the ceiling) explored the pattern of the structure for the projecting deck.

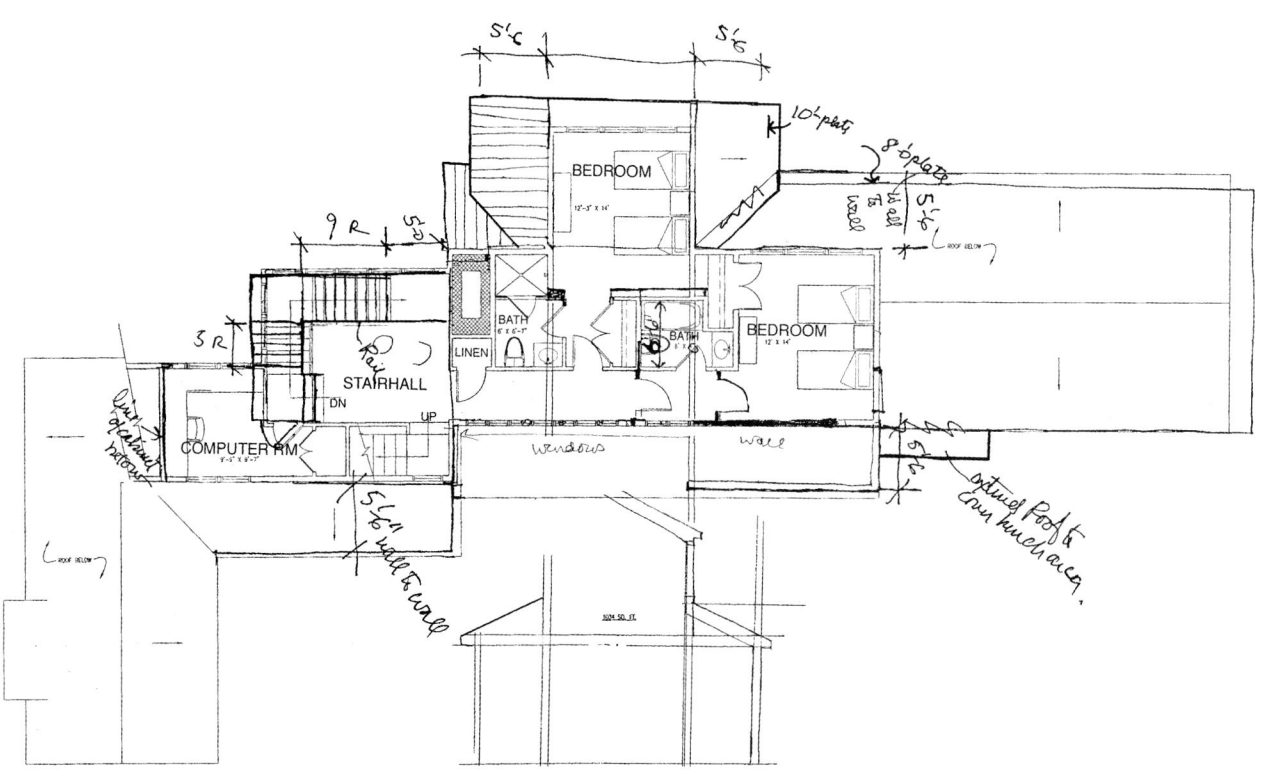

Figure 54 Second floor

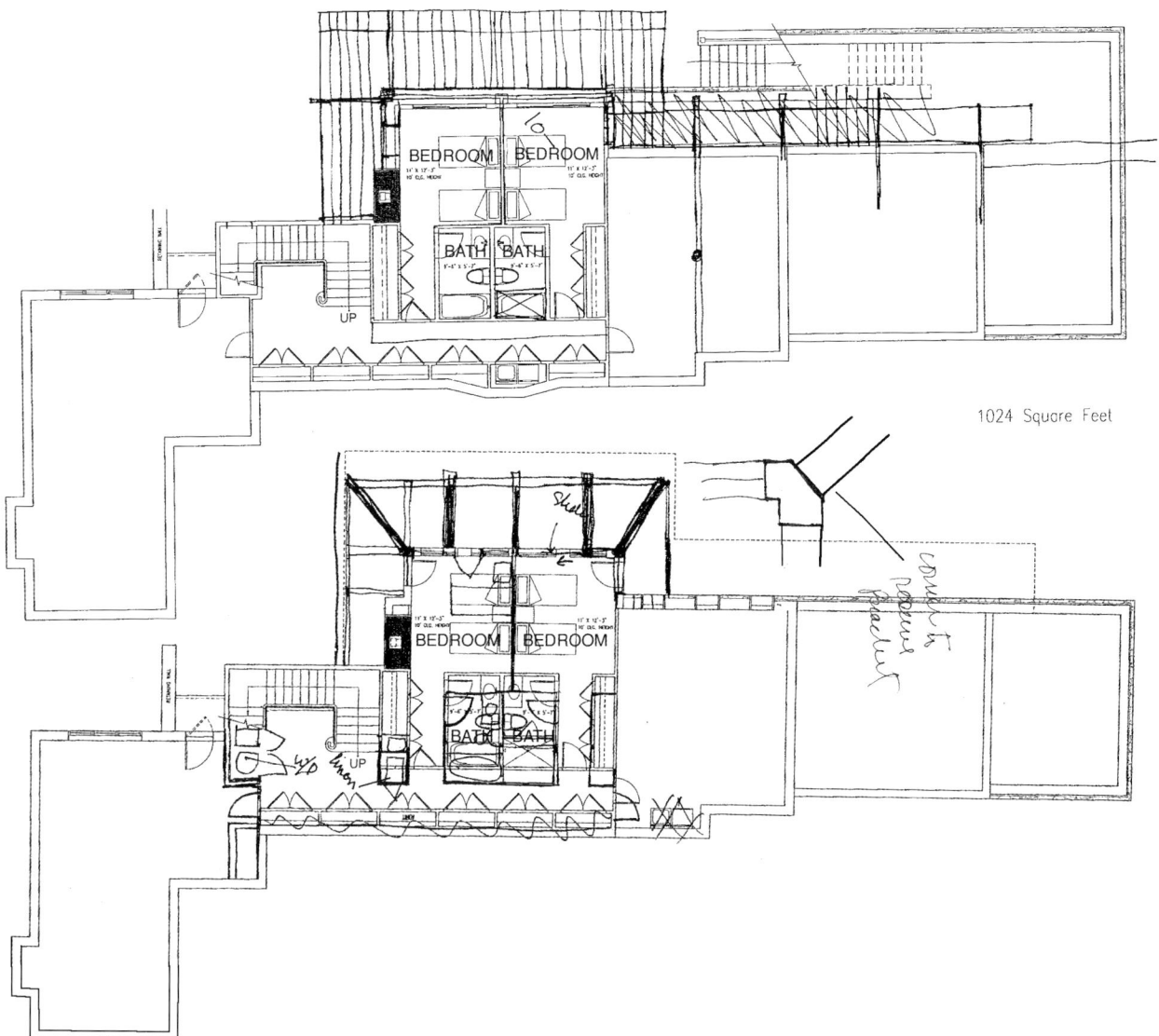

Figure 55 Ground floor

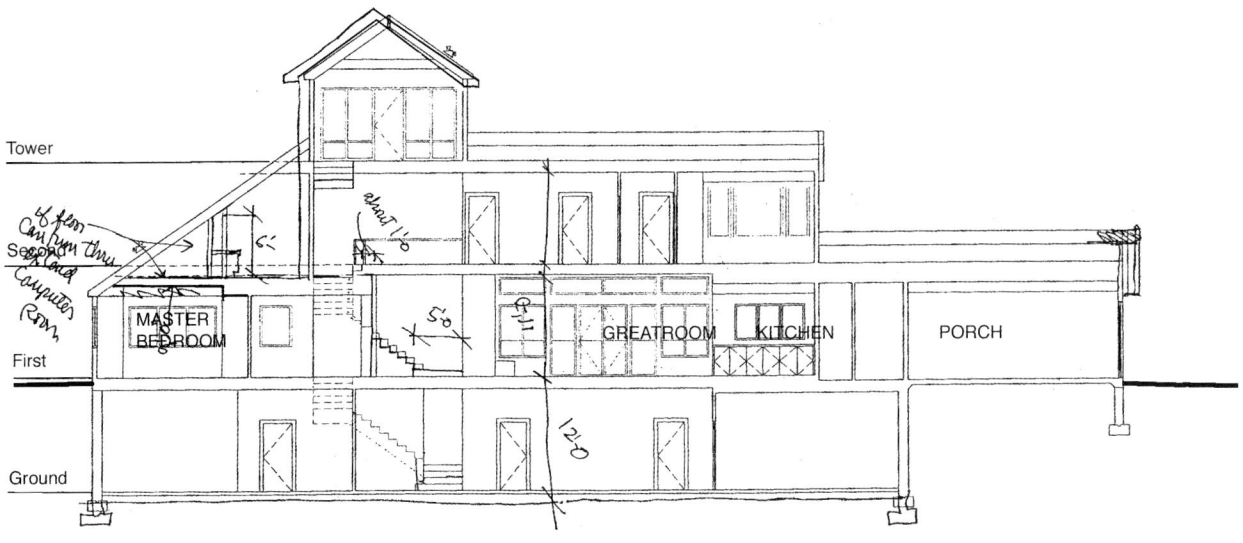

Figure 56

With the plans suitably resolved, I updated sections and elevations on the computer. Sections confirmed the appropriateness of vertical dimensions and reconfirmed accurate floor-to-floor relationships. Roof slopes were adjusted to accommodate desired eave heights and upper floor window heads, ceiling heights were set, and window fenestration patterns were attuned. A section focused on the flue from the great room fireplace. It was reconfigured so that its projection above the roof would have less impact on views from the tower. A metal flue provided the least obstruction, and its appearance worked well with the utilitarian aesthetic of the house.

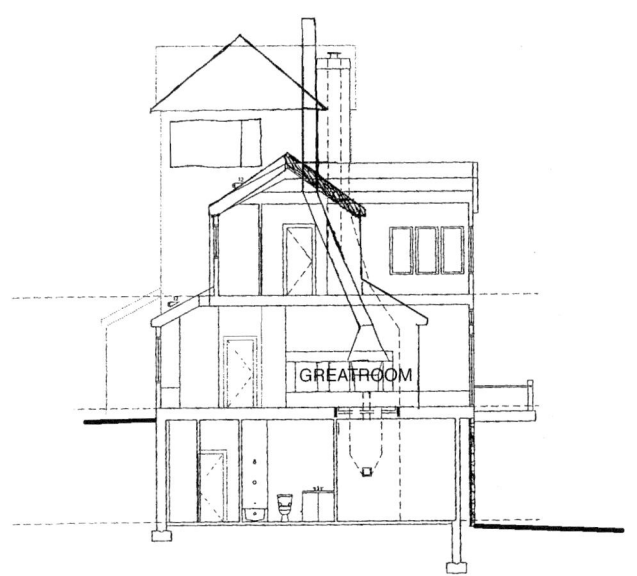

Figure 56 East–west longitudinal section (top); section through great room looking towards fireplace (bottom)

Figure 57 South elevation (top); north elevation (bottom)

Figure 57

I reviewed and marked up computer drawings of the elevations to improve proportions. Illustrations for window openings were fine-tuned and I reviewed details (such as how to secure the metal chimney flue) to ensure their consistency with the aesthetics of the house.

Figure 58 North elevation

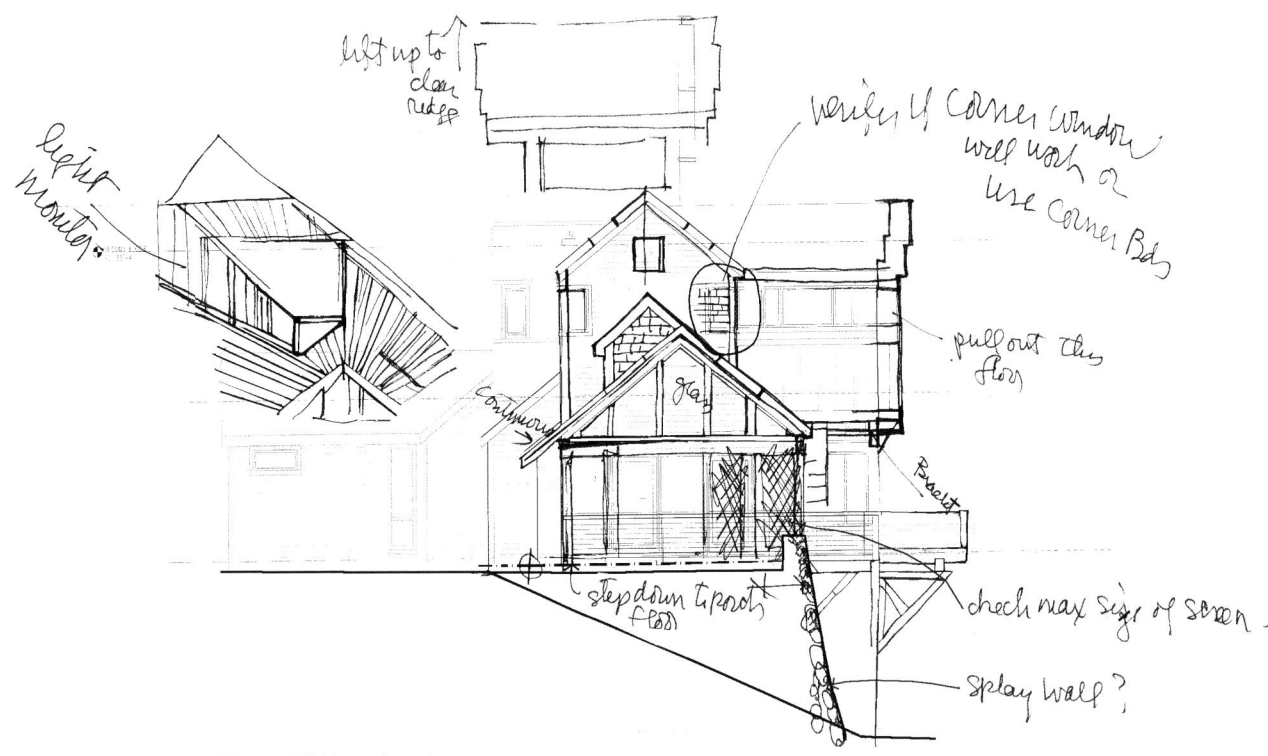

Figure 59 East elevation

Figures 58 and 59

Some decisions were now finalized:

- a metal roof with its attendant rib pattern was selected for its fireproof qualities, its ease of maintenance, and its consistency with the indigenous expression of the house
- red cedar shingles were selected as the siding material. My intention was to course shingles with two wide bands, alternating with a narrow one, creating a broader overall shingle pattern in scale with the size of the house
- I extended the gable roof ends out beyond the walls of the house to give wet-weather protection to high gable windows and to provide further sun screening on the south. These extensions would also ensure deeper shadows and a more sculptural quality to the façade
- a portion of the second floor bedroom area was pulled out as an overhang to provide wet-weather protection for the expansive glass window wall of the great room below and slightly more space for the second floor bedroom
- I proposed a clerestory monitor on the porch roof to admit more southern light into its high ceiling space and to moderate the mass of the porch for a better visual transition to the rest of the house

Figure 60 Model view from southeast

Figure 61 Model view from north

Figure 62 Model view from southeast

Figure 63 Model view from northern slope

Figure 64 Aerial model view from east

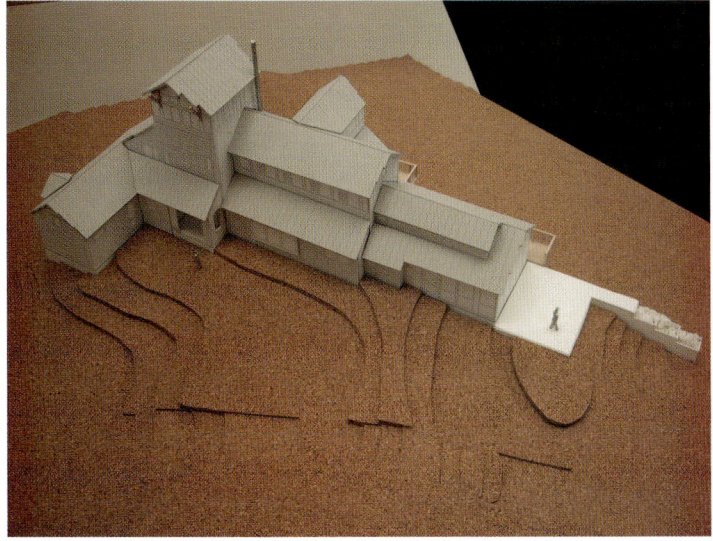

Figure 65 Aerial model view from south–southwest

Figure 66 Model view from northwest

Figures 60–66

Now that I was sufficiently comfortable with the form of the house, a scale model was constructed. It was a useful, three-dimensional tool for confirming that the design met my objectives. If not, I would revise, rework and modify the model.

I reviewed the model to ensure that there was a sense of unity and coherence to the house—that the parts fit together comfortably and there was simplicity in the design, but with sufficient variation to provide interest. I wanted to make sure that the house fit the site and related to surrounding grades. I felt assured that it sat comfortably on the site and was expressive of its location, the scale was residential (not too grand or monumental), roof pitches and overhangs were appropriate, and intersections workable, and windows and doors were proportioned to the overall form and were located to function meaningfully with interior spaces. But I needed to make several modifications:

- I simplified the roof form by redesigning the master bath and removing the bathtub extension from the side of the house
- I expanded the southwestern great room window vertically to admit more sunlight and provide better views up the mountainside, and added a horizontal sun visor to help control glare and provide shadow patterns on the bright southwestern elevations
- I removed the wall brackets supporting the projecting deck and expressed the deck as a cantilevered element. This change allowed better headroom below and a more simple and direct visual expression. The model further exposed the importance of making the railing enclosing the deck as light and transparent as possible to provide the unimpeded view I had wanted to achieve. In the final drawings, it was detailed as a series of thin steel plate stanchions, which supported horizontal cables and was topped with a wooden cap rail

Figure 67

Revisions were reflected in the elevations and incorporated in ongoing drawings. With these final adjustments incorporated, I felt comfortable with the design of the house. There would always be refinements to be made, but the spatial configuration and organization of the house had now been established, and its shape and materials substantially fixed. It met my client's objectives and my own aspirations. Alternatives had been studied effectively and I felt that ongoing decisions would fit within the design parameters that had been established.

The design would now be developed into a set of construction documents. This entailed:

- working out the details of structural, mechanical, electrical and plumbing systems
- defining specific types of finish materials and selecting colors for walls, floors and ceiling
- detailing the workings of the fireplace, stairway, kitchen and cabinetry
- selecting specific doors, windows, hardware and lighting fixtures
- choosing furniture and furnishings
- detailing the enclosure to ensure weather tightness and constructability

A final set of drawings was produced that became the basis of the construction contract. When substantial construction of the house was completed, paint colors were selected, furniture and furnishings installed, and finished landscape materials put in place. My clients, their children and friends are now happily using the house. It has become a home.

Figure 67 South elevation (top); north elevation (bottom)

IMPLEMENTING THE DESIGN: The Completed House

> Creativity is allowing yourself to make mistakes. Art is knowing which ones to keep.
>
> **Scott Adams**

As mentioned in the introduction to this book, heuristics are rules of thumb that grow out of our prior experiences and help steer our judgment. They are useful strategies, which may not always be faultless, but generally prove successful.

While designing, I am not aware of calling upon these rules. I simply act intuitively on what I think is appropriate. Unconsciously, however, these principles form the basis of what I do and the design decisions that I make.

In this study, I have made an effort to articulate these guidelines. Some are easy to verbalize such as "Design to a human scale" or "Design spaces to maximize views." But others are more difficult to put into words. For instance, "Create a house fitting to its unique location by conveying in the form of the house distinct qualities or characteristics expressive of its site" is a subtle and more complex design idea.

Architecture, as any art form, is so much more than words and definitions. As the poet Robert Frost succinctly put it, "Poetry is what evaporates in translation." Nevertheless, the process of trying to articulate these rules of thumb has helped me understand how I think and what influences my design. Where I have been able to put them into words, I have an added check on the appropriateness of my design principles and an opportunity to reevaluate my objectives. Perhaps an awareness of these guidelines may help others comprehend and improve their own design capabilities as well.

- Site the house to take advantage of views, sunlight and prevailing breezes.
- Carefully consider the landform so that the home will fit appropriately on the site.
- Convey in the visual quality of the house the special nature of the site and program.
- Be minimally disruptive to the landform.
- Preserve trees.
- Locate the house being mindful of the need to link up to existing pedestrian and vehicular access ways adjacent to the site.
- Set floor elevations to balance cut and fill, and high enough to allow water to drain away from the house.
- Design spaces to be appropriately sized, configured and detailed, to graciously accommodate the activities expected to take place within them.
- Create space and form that is expressive of function and use.
- Incorporate unobstructed circulation flow with visual cues, such as views to the surroundings, to provide a clear sense of orientation.
- Zone the house to separate public from private areas, and provide appropriate levels of visual and acoustic privacy.
- Provide spatial variety and, where appropriate, clear spatial definition.
- Design to a human scale. Where appropriate reduce perceived massiveness by articulating the overall form into smaller components.
- Design spaces to maximize views, admit appropriate sunlight and control glare.
- In addition to maximizing views to the exterior, design for vistas within the house.
- Design for cross ventilation and proper airflow.

- Provide easy accessibility to outdoor living.
- Design spaces to be adaptable to future changes in lifestyle. Provide some spatial redundancy, for example, more than one wall surface so that furniture arrangements can change over time.
- Try to think three-dimensionally as you arrange a plan so that you can imagine and visualize the potential of a space.
- Reduce perceived height by overhanging eaves and defined cornices.
- Create a unified composition with each component reinforcing and sustaining the central conception.
- Manipulate spaces and form to provide interest and delight. Balance orderliness and visual clarity with the unexpected and unanticipated.
- Let form evolve and express its function.
- Be straightforward and direct, avoid pretentiousness and strive for fresh and unimitative solutions.
- Be cognizant of the need for security. Avoid hiding places, particularly on the exterior.
- Be conscious of conditions that offer opportunities for energy conservation and preservation of natural resources.
- Provide unifying transitions to reinforce the intent of the overall composition
- Take clues from indigenous architecture in selecting exterior cladding materials friendly to local weather conditions and local building techniques. Be conscious of resale and marketability needs.
- Design with cost and constructability in mind.
- Think about how daylight will affect and enrich the appearance of the form of the house and the character of its spaces. Use this understanding to reinforce and enhance desired visual qualities. For example, use recesses, offsets, setbacks, projections and overhangs, as well as textures and patterns to reinforce and enhance the form and space by contrasting bright and reflective light with dark and recessive shade and shadow.
- To further capture the enrichment that light will bring, be conscious of appropriate materials ranging from opaque and reflective to transparent and translucent.
- Be open to a wide range of ideas. Don't be critical too quickly, as seemingly inappropriate ideas may trigger useful and unforeseen possibilities.
- Be open to negative client responses to your suggestions. Listening carefully may lead to even better ideas.

Opposite The screen porch, with its roof monitor, captures the southern light and opens into a grass terrace with shading trees

Left Sitting just below the tree line, the house looks out over a flowering meadow and the Berkshire Mountains beyond. Its massing and form reflect the clustering trees among which it has been placed

Above The house securely rooted in the sloping mountainside. The shape of the house and its fenestration responds to, and expresses, the distinctive nature of the space within

Opposite top View from the east

Opposite bottom View from the north

87

Left View from the northwest: The pitched roofs express their protective nature and visually reduce the two-story scale of the house. The L-shaped form helps tie back and anchor the house to the sloping mountainside. Cantilevered decks project out over a grassy knoll, providing unobstructed views of the surrounding countryside

Above The entrance, informal and unobtrusive, affords a protective transition from the natural environment to the built spaces within. Semi-enclosed for weather protection, the space encloses a built-in bench to aid in removing boots and winter garments

Above Arriving by car, the setting of the house hints at the magnificent views from within

Opposite Distant view to the house set into the mountainside

Above From the south, the house nestles into the mountainside. Its screened-in porch and terrace take advantage of the southern exposure

Opposite The screened-in porch, from within with its roof monitor, captures the southern light and opens onto a grass terrace. Glass panels can replace screens to provide extended use in cooler weather and protection during winter months

Above The living room opens onto a cantilevered deck with vistas to the surrounding countryside

Opposite top A long view through the living room, kitchen, mudroom and porch. Long views within the home supplement views to the outside and, through changing, unexpected light conditions, provide variety and interest as one moves about the house

Opposite bottom The living area with its indigenous stone fireplace and corner windows provides a panoramic view to the valley below

Top Although open to the activities taking place within the living area, the kitchen is treated as a distinct space—an alcove adjacent to the living area

Right and opposite Large glass areas designed for the southern side of the house capture and diffuse sunlight while providing views up the mountainside

Left The master bedroom with a window seat looking out over the valley
Above Entering a bedroom with a glancing view to the countryside

Right Bird's-eye view in winter

Additional Examples

This chapter presents photographs and plans of some additional homes we at CBT have designed which are also examples of how architectural space and form have been influenced by heuristics.

House in Woods Hole

This Cape Cod residence sits atop a hill with views overlooking Nantucket Sound and Buzzards Bay. Part of a shingle-style Cape Cod locality, the house borrows traditional Cape Cod forms and materials, adapting them for a contemporary lifestyle and enabling the house to fit compatibly with the surrounding neighborhood homes. White cedar shingle siding weathered to a warm grey, red cedar shingle roofs, white painted trim and fieldstone walls are all part of the Cape Cod architectural vocabulary for the house. The wrap-around porch, with its wide, overhanging roof, is a wonderful place for outdoor living, providing weather protection and sun control for the living spaces within.

- Take clues from indigenous architecture in selecting building materials responsive to local weather conditions, building techniques and availability.
- Consider surrounding architecture and be responsive to it, where appropriate, such as in a historic district.
- Design spaces to maximize views, admit appropriate sunlight and control glare.

Right Aerial view: house sits atop a hill with its turreted bay providing panoramic views of Nantucket Sound and Buzzards Bay

Top Evening

Bottom View of the house from the south showing protective nature of the wrap-around porch

Opposite Detail showing indigenous cape cod materials: fieldstone chimney and walls, red cedar shingle roof, white cedar siding weathering light gray, white painted trim and wrap around porch

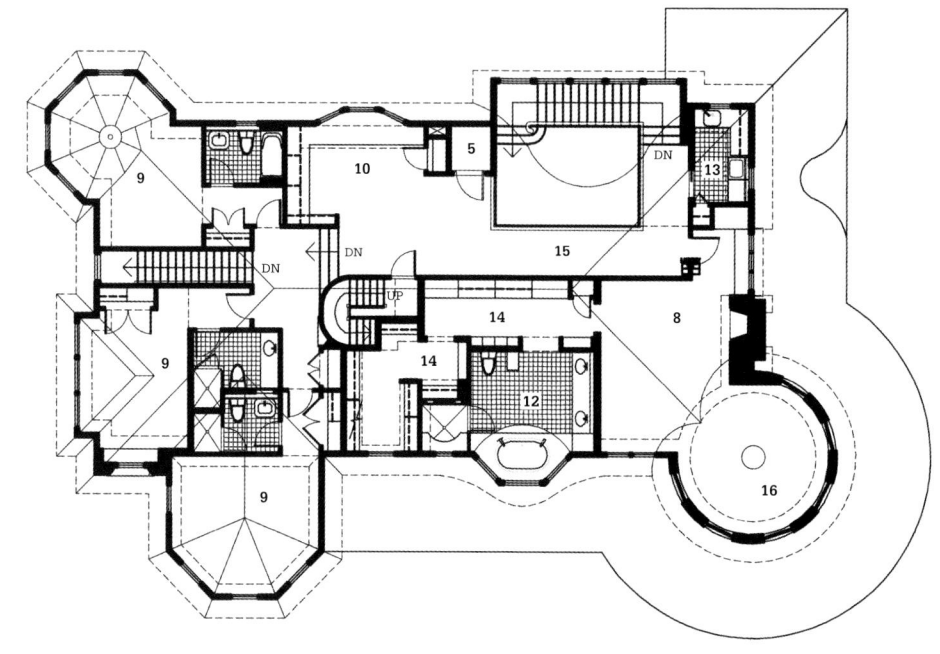

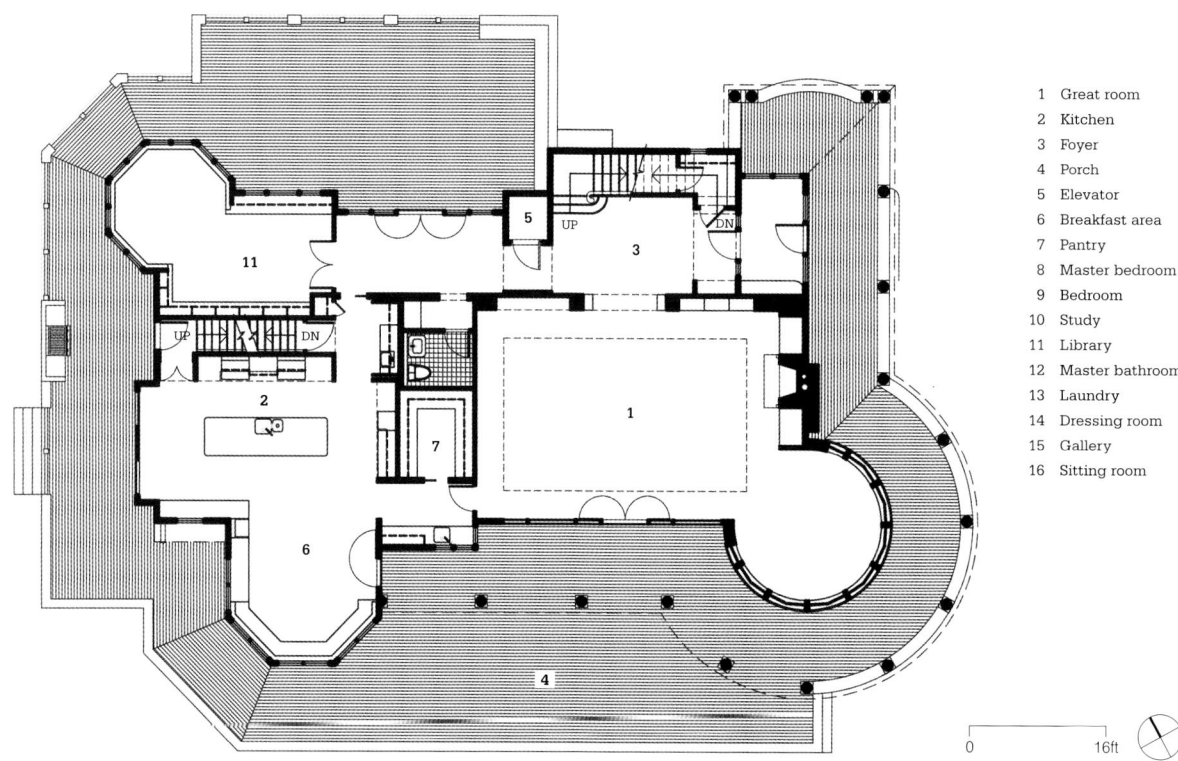

1 Great room
2 Kitchen
3 Foyer
4 Porch
5 Elevator
6 Breakfast area
7 Pantry
8 Master bedroom
9 Bedroom
10 Study
11 Library
12 Master bathroom
13 Laundry
14 Dressing room
15 Gallery
16 Sitting room

Interior space has been designed to graciously accommodate all the activities normally associated with residential living. In addition, careful consideration was given to the owners' art collection. Space was provided, and special accommodations were created, to display various art objects in an unobtrusive and unpretentious way.

- Design spaces that are appropriately sized, configured and detailed, to graciously accommodate the activities expected to take place within them.

Opposite top Second floor plan

Opposite bottom First floor plan

Above Looking toward the foyer from the great room

House in Weston

Just as solid and transparent surfaces, walls, windows and doors must be arranged to create spaces and accommodate needs on the interior of the house, so must they be studied and positioned to meet functional and aesthetic purposes on the exterior.

This photograph of a house in a suburb of Boston is a typical example of how this concurrence of internal and external conditions can be successfully accomplished.

The process is similar to that of a painter composing a canvas with the added requirement that the composition of the exterior elevations must also satisfy interior conditions not visible on the exterior.

On the elevation shown here, two gabled roof forms, shaped to correspond to the width of spaces within the house, have been symmetrically positioned around a central axis. This axis is centered on the main entrance, giving the entrance special importance so that it is easily identified. Two upper story windows framed by brackets (to subtly distinguish them from the third window) align with, and reinforce, this central axis. The entrance is shown as a recessed, sheltered place given more visual importance by its uniquely arched form and detached columns. On the left gabled form, windows are placed aligning with one another and with the centerline of the gable in a straightforward and ordered way.

Left Entrance elevation from the east

However, on the right gable, a two story semicircular bay is offset from the gable's centerline but is visually balanced on the left side of the elevation by a smaller, upper-story cupola—pushed further to the left of the central axis to help visually oppose and counterweight the larger, two-story bay on the right side.

Composing the elevation is a balance between creating order, coherence and predictability on the one hand, and variety, complexity and the unexpected on the other. Too much order can become boring, but too much complexity is chaos.

In the photograph shown here, a balance is established. An ordered composition has been created by: the symmetrical arrangement of the gable roofs and the location of the central entrance, the simplicity of roof forms, the consistency of the shingle coursing on the façade, and the uniformity of the windows in size, style, color and common sill height.

Variety, as well as the unanticipated, are needed to give the composition life and vitality: the odd shape and uniqueness of the cantilevered cupola, the unexpected offset of the semicircular bay (not on the center of the gable), the placement of a third, unsymmetrical window above the entrance, the added variety of windows with transoms (indicating more special places within), the shifting manner windows are mounted—some continuous with painted mullions, others arranged as 'punched' windows because they appear pushed into the shingle surface. One might call some of these moves mistakes, but their inconsistency actually adds vitality to the façade. Properly executed, these 'mistakes' turn out to be win-win conditions. They enable the needs of the interiors to be resolved while, through their spontaneity, give vitality to the exterior elevation.

- Manipulate spaces and form to provide interest and delight. Balance orderliness and visual clarity with the unexpected and unanticipated.
- Design to a human scale—consider reducing perceived massiveness by articulating the overall form into smaller components.
- Create a unified composition with each component reinforcing and sustaining the central conception.

Top Entrance elevation from the driveway
Opposite top Second floor plan
Opposite bottom First floor plan

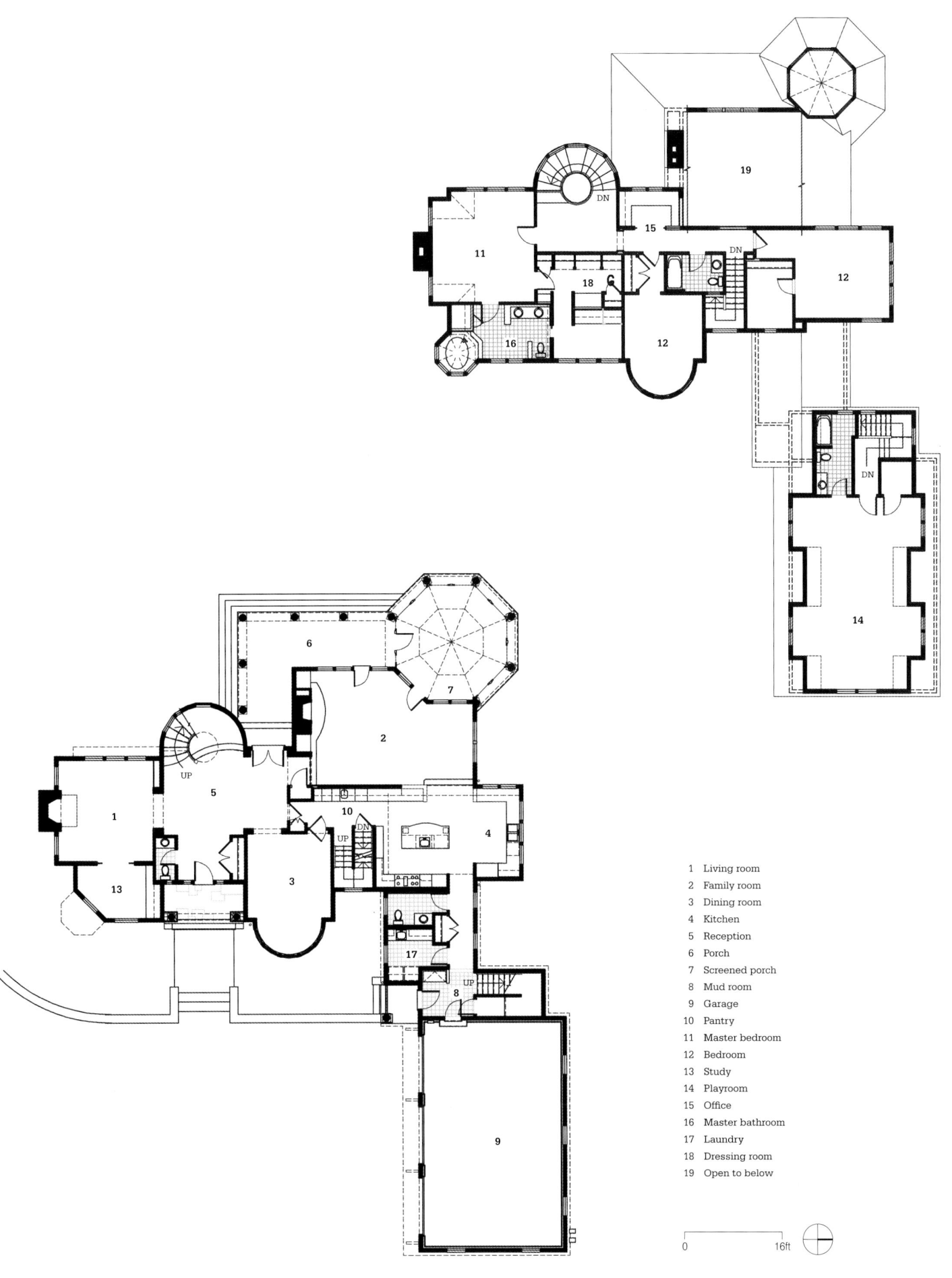

House in Dartmouth

Located in a rural area of southeastern Massachusetts, this house is sited to take advantage of views of an adjacent river that meanders along its northern border. The plan of the house responds to the shifting direction of the river, with spaces rotating to maximize the differing views. The composition of the house is expressed as a series of small, connected structures, which help reduce the scale of the house and recall indigenous farm buildings prevalent in the area.

- To create a unique house exclusive to its location, convey in the form of the house distinctive qualities or characteristics of its site.

Left Aerial view showing the orientation of the house to the adjacent river

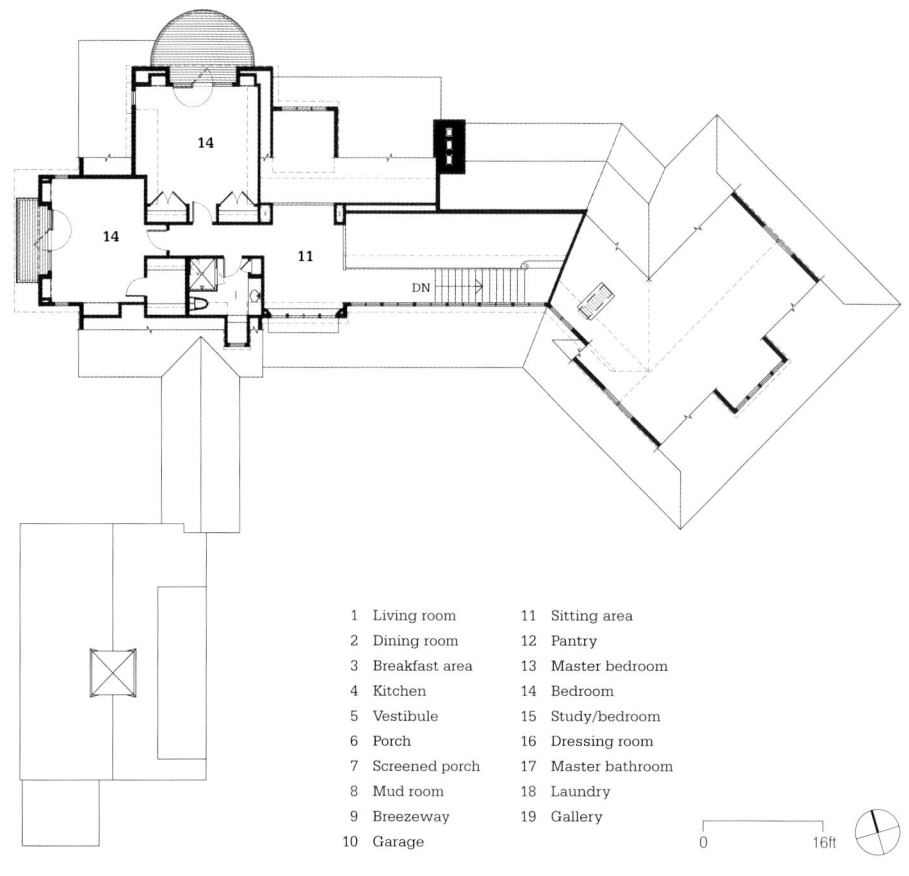

1 Living room
2 Dining room
3 Breakfast area
4 Kitchen
5 Vestibule
6 Porch
7 Screened porch
8 Mud room
9 Breezeway
10 Garage
11 Sitting area
12 Pantry
13 Master bedroom
14 Bedroom
15 Study/bedroom
16 Dressing room
17 Master bathroom
18 Laundry
19 Gallery

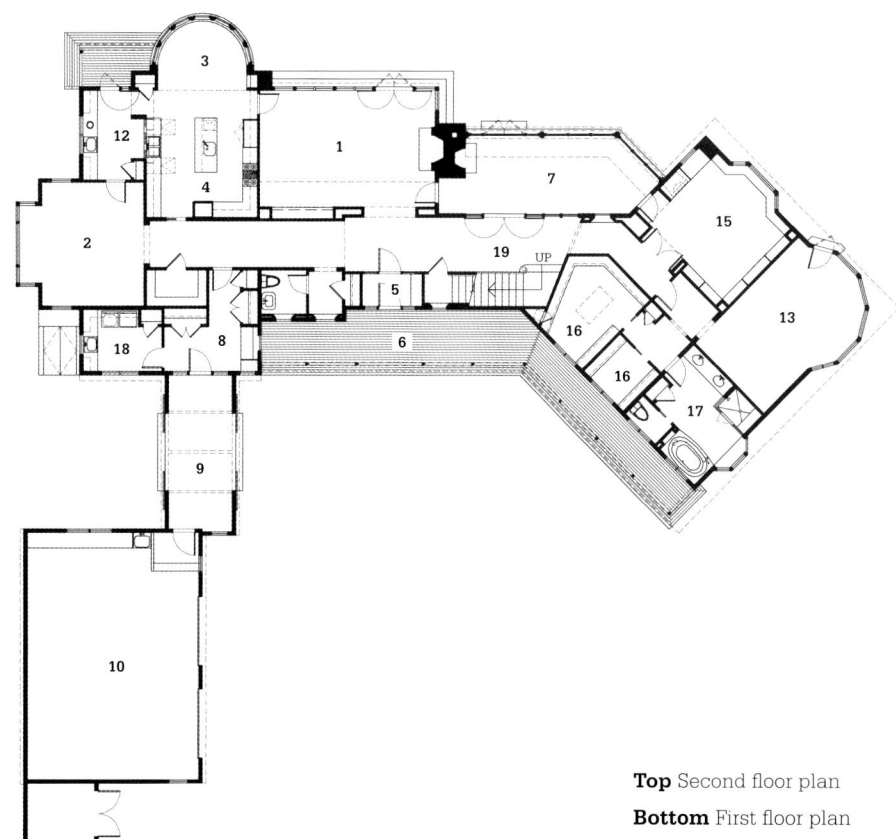

Top Second floor plan

Bottom First floor plan

Opposite View from the breezeway looking to the entry porch. Note the south facing clerestory windows bringing southern light into the north-facing house

A covered porch on the front, southern side of the house, along with a breezeway that connects the home to its garage, helps define a protected entrance courtyard. A cat-sized copy of the front doorway adds a personal touch to the feline friendly home.

- Be cognizant of the importance of a gracious, welcoming, and protective entrance.

Although views to the river are to the north, clerestory windows on the south side of the house infuse the north facing spaces with light and sun and also enable natural cross ventilation.

- Design spaces to maximize views and benefit from friendly southern sunlight.

Opposite The entry gallery looking toward the dining room. High clerestory windows aided by glass transoms introduce friendly southern sunlight to the north facing rooms

Top The sunset light casts deep shadows on the façade looking out to the river

Left Looking from the entry gallery through the living room to views of the river beyond

House in Mattapoisett

Designed as the summer home for a family of four, this house sits on a small offshore island on the coast of Massachusetts. Approached by means of a narrow causeway, the house is oriented to take advantage of spectacular views and sited to shelter selected outdoor spaces from prevailing southwesterly winds.

- Site the house to take advantage of views and southerly sun. Be cognizant of, and shield outdoor living spaces from, prevailing winds.

The house is designed to contrast with the almost never-ending, horizontal nature of the surrounding ocean. With its steeply pitched roofs and wide porches, it reflects its commanding location while taking advantage of the panoramic views.

- Convey in the image of the house the special nature of its site and program.

The plan of the house is a cruciform, with spaces that radiate out from a central mechanical core. This shape is reminiscent of a simple pyramidal form. Each side varies slightly, responding to its orientation and the functional changes taking place within—a theme with variations.

- Strive for a clarifying conceptual organization that can help give order to dissimilar elements.

Right Aerial view showing island house and its commanding location

Above View from south

Opposite top Second floor plan and getaway

Opposite bottom First floor plan

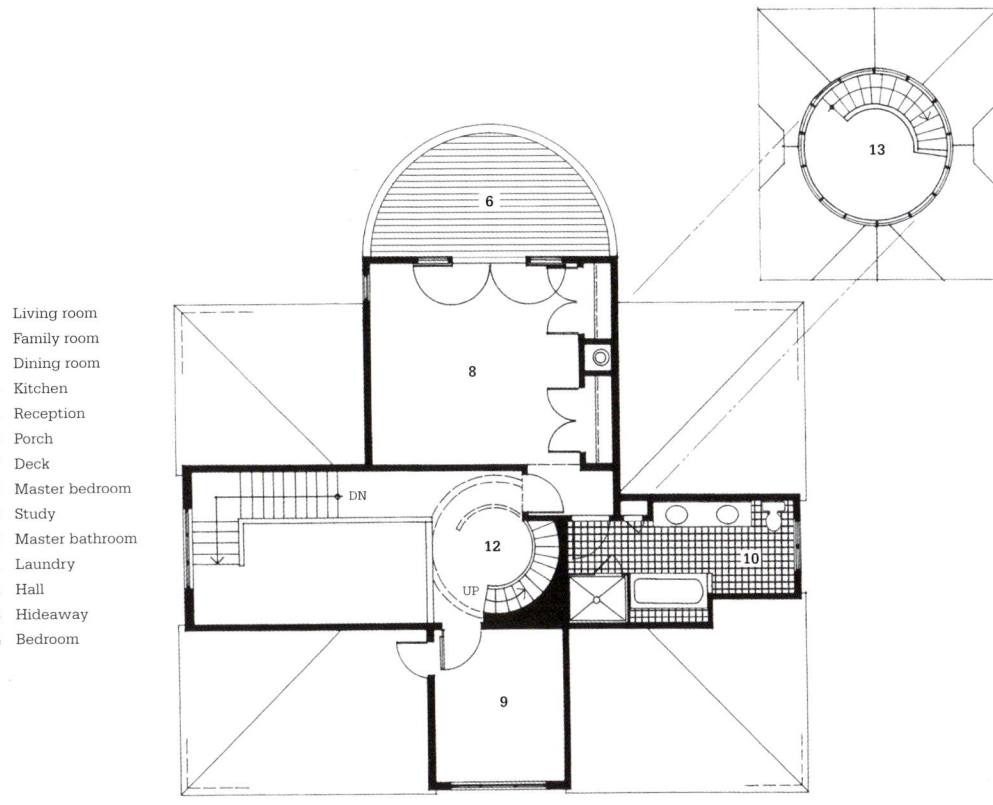

1 Living room
2 Family room
3 Dining room
4 Kitchen
5 Reception
6 Porch
7 Deck
8 Master bedroom
9 Study
10 Master bathroom
11 Laundry
12 Hall
13 Hideaway
14 Bedroom

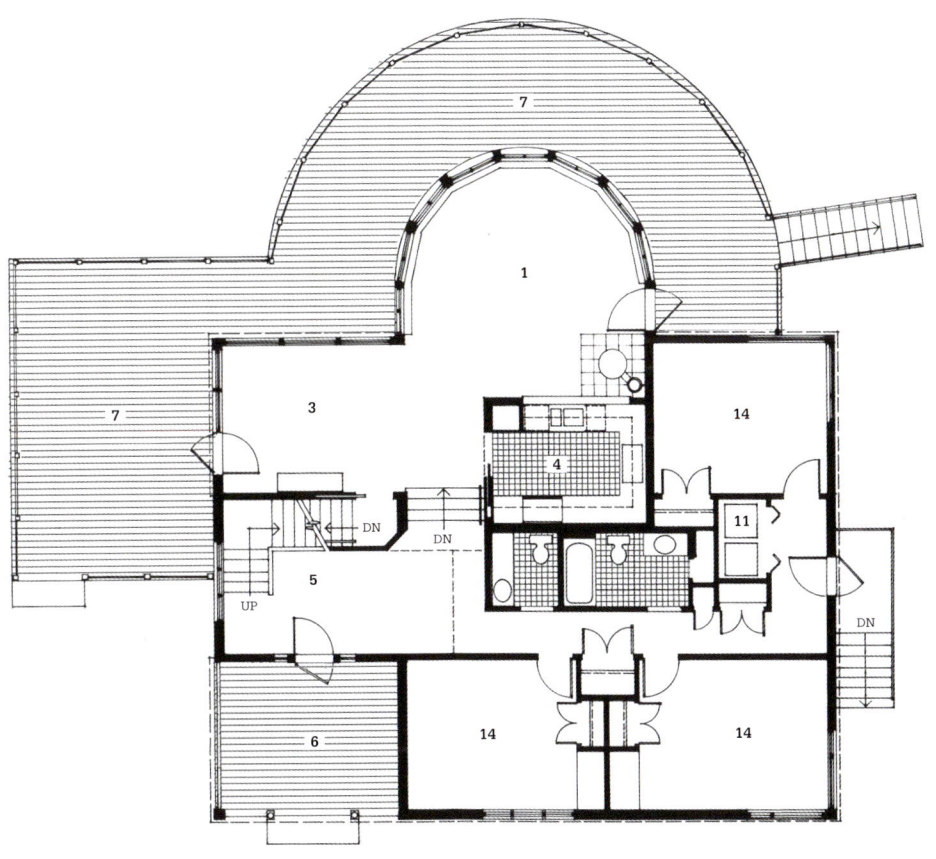

The floor levels of the house step down the site, carefully responding to, and respecting, existing grades while enabling more active areas of the house to profit by higher ceilings.

- Carefully consider the landform. Design the house to fit comfortably with the site.

Emerging from the center of the roof is a lookout tower, which affords 360-degree views. This space is also a natural ventilator, allowing warmer air to be eliminated from the house as cooler air is pulled in from below.

- Be conscious of conditions that offer opportunities for energy conservation.

Above Evening from the west

Opposite top Living room with its panoramic views

Opposite bottom Dining area looking out through the living area

House on Martha's Vineyard

This house sits in a wooded site on Martha's Vineyard, an island off the coast of Massachusetts. It has long water views to a great pond. Zoning restrictions in this location limited the height of the house to one story. The form of the house is a response to this limiting constraint, with dormer windows and windowed gable roof ends enabling upper level access to distant water views. A long entry drive winds through the woods, arriving at an entrance courtyard.

The house is broken into three components: the main living area, a bedroom wing, and a garage and workshop area, which wrap to form an arrival courtyard. Breaking the mass of the house into smaller parts helped reduce its scale, enabling the house to fit comfortably into its wooded setting and also permitting each section of the house to be independently oriented in a direction that maximized best water views.

High spaces utilizing the volume within the roof and changes in floor level help to create a variety of spatial experiences.

- Provide spatial variety and design spaces to be appropriately sized, configured and detailed, to properly accommodate the activities expected to take place within them.
- Design to a human scale. Consider reducing perceived massiveness by articulating the overall form into smaller components.
- Zone the house to separate public from private areas. Provide appropriate levels of visual and acoustic privacy.

Right Entrance court

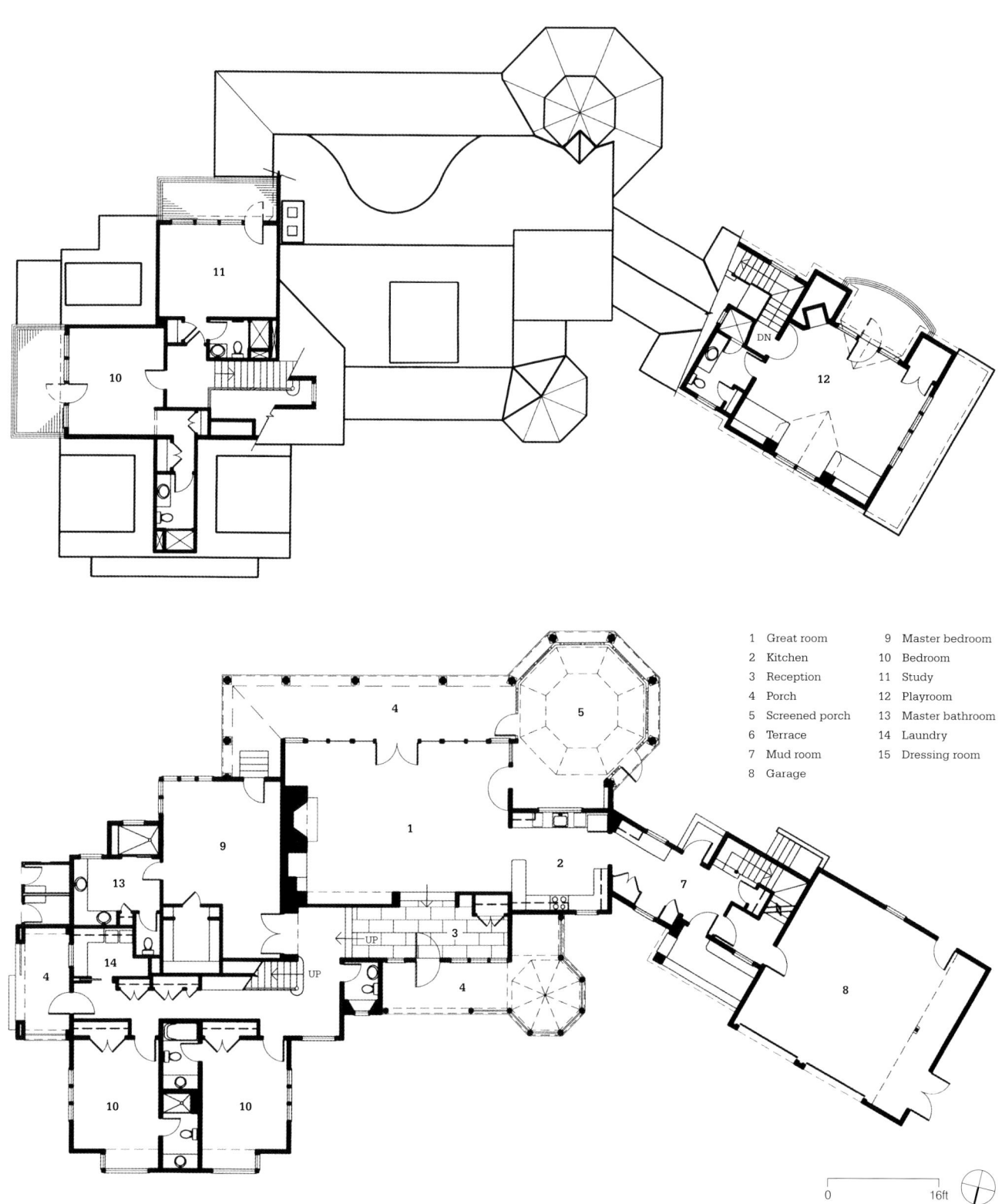

1	Great room	9	Master bedroom
2	Kitchen	10	Bedroom
3	Reception	11	Study
4	Porch	12	Playroom
5	Screened porch	13	Master bathroom
6	Terrace	14	Laundry
7	Mud room	15	Dressing room
8	Garage		

Top Second floor plan

Bottom First floor plan

Opposite The great room

Opposite top View from the south

Opposite bottom Evening view

Above The covered porch looking out to great pond

House in the Berkshire Mountains

For this house in the mountains of western Massachusetts, red cedar shingles were selected as the siding material for the exterior walls. Shingles were selected for many reasons, including their weathering ability, ease of use, textural quality, soft natural color and indigenous character. In addition, wall surfaces made of shingles have the unique ability to conform to various shapes, to curve and to twist. This distinctive characteristic enabled the wall forms to be more organic and sculptural. Wall surfaces were warped to shed water and curved to form protective overhangs. The enclosing wall surface of the living room, for example, bows out to facilitate panoramic views from within. This curving shape is facilitated and protected by a sheltering roof, formed by the protruding shingled wall above. Curved shingled surfaces also easily enclosed the semicircular stairway and the projecting bay windows.

- Select materials to meet functional needs. Then express these materials in ways that visually reinforce or exploit their inherent qualities.

Another example of this heuristic is the way stone piers supporting the overhanging deck express their function. Stone can be put to use in many ways. As a paving material, for example, it can be installed flat and smooth. Used in this way, the image of the stone is one of hardness and durability. For the piers, however, each individual stone is articulated. Each is arranged and set using deeply recessed mortar joints. Designed in this way, the bulk and mass of the stone material is highlighted, and its ability to support the heavy load above is expressed.

Right Southwest elevation looking out over the mountainside

134

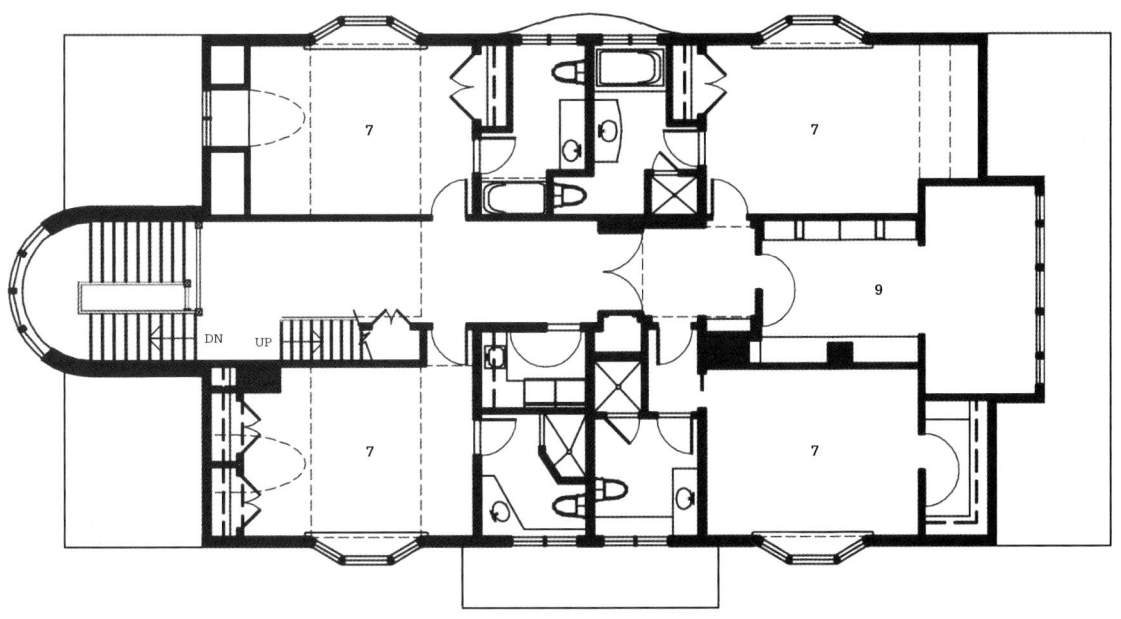

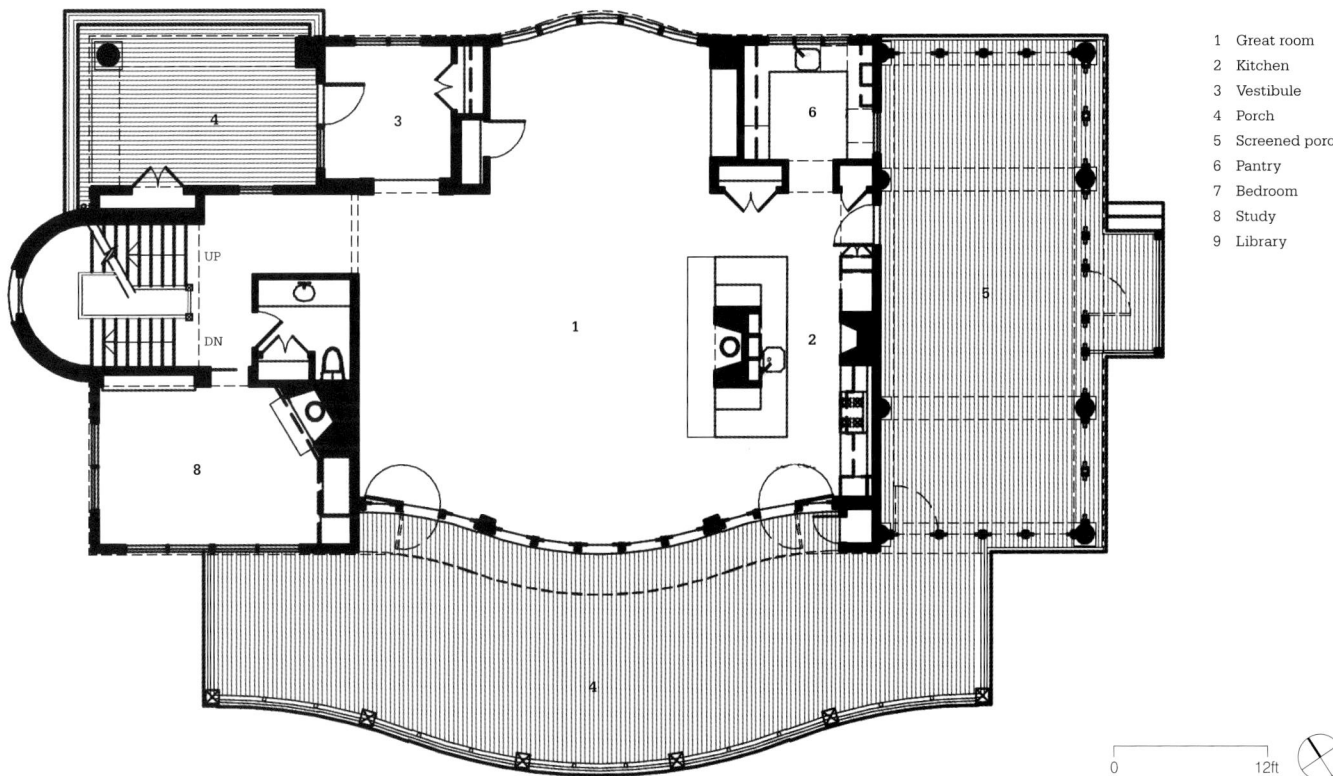

1 Great room
2 Kitchen
3 Vestibule
4 Porch
5 Screened porch
6 Pantry
7 Bedroom
8 Study
9 Library

Opposite top The entrance porch and stair overlook

Opposite bottom left The interior of the stair from the first floor

Opposite bottom right The screened-in porch

Top Second floor plan

Bottom First floor plan

In this vacation home, a large multipurpose living area—a congregating space for family and friends—was a desired objective. There was, however, a wish to separate the clutter of the kitchen from this space. Although, that exclusion came with the concern that whoever was in the kitchen would be left out of conversations. The solution became a visual screen that masked the kitchen and its clutter but allowed those cooking to continue to partake in activities. The screen was an open, freestanding fireplace set in the center of the living area with built-in kitchen facilities concealed behind.

- Look beyond the norm to find design solutions that will optimize your clients' objectives.

Top The fireplace divider from the kitchen side
Bottom Standing in the kitchen area looking out to the view
Opposite The great room with its fireplace divider screening the kitchen from the living area

House in Chestnut Hill

This house is located in the Chestnut Hill area of Newton, Massachusetts. A portion of the structure was originally the carriage house for an adjacent estate. It was converted to a residence in the 1960s. A portion of the 1960s building was retained, but the structure was gutted and renovated to accommodate new additions that transformed the house into a gracious and livable contemporary residence.

The form of the house wraps to create a vehicular entrance court.

- Consider the process of arriving at the house in a vehicle as well as arriving by foot. Plan for a welcoming and gracious arrival process that accommodates the needs of both.

A circular structure containing the dining room below and the master bedroom above occupies the highest point on the site, providing commanding views over the surrounding landscaped gardens.

Right View of the house from the southwest

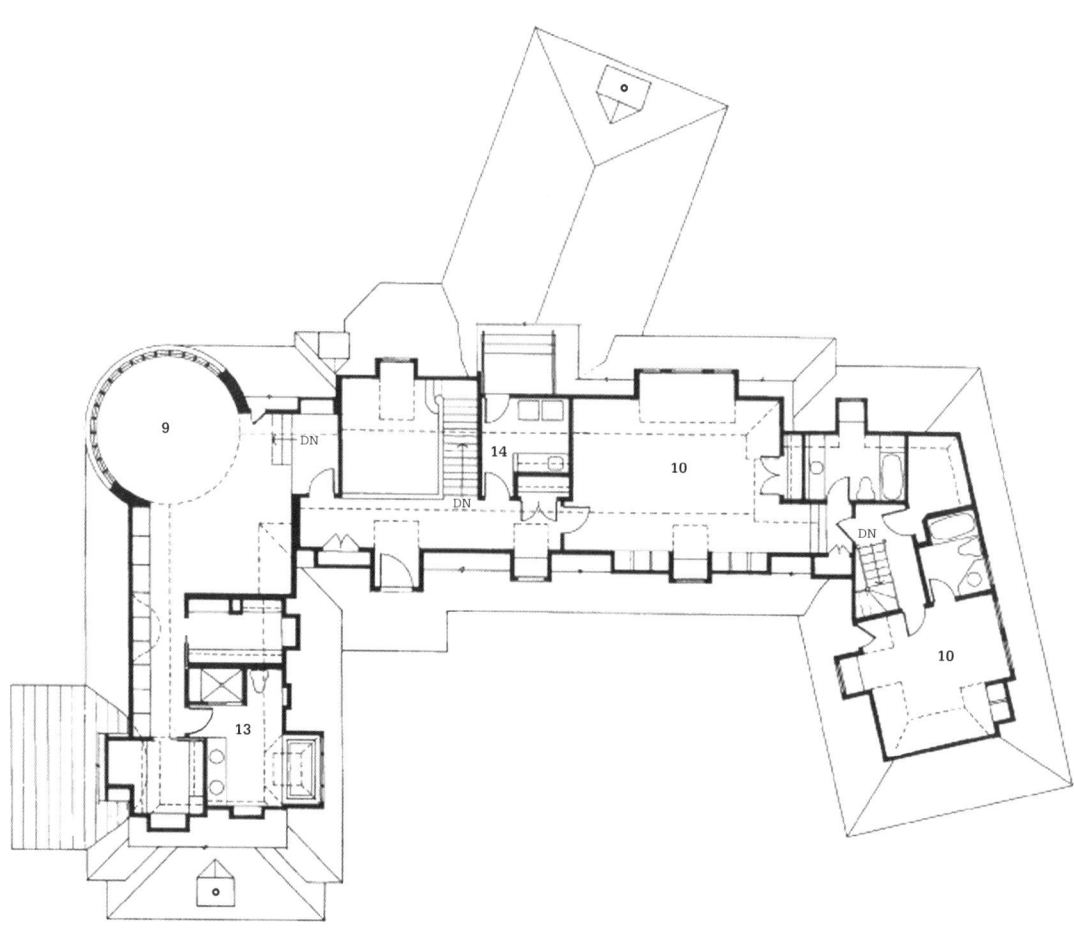
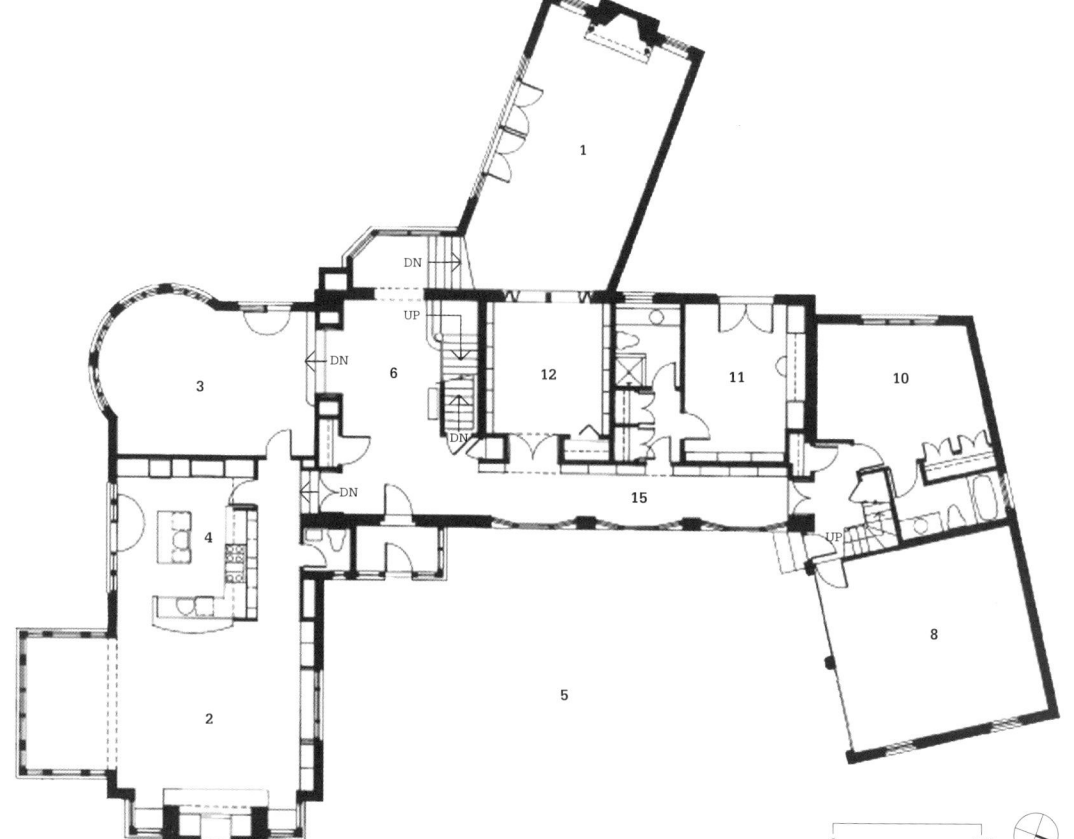

1 Living room
2 Family room
3 Dining room
4 Kitchen
5 Entry court
6 Reception
7 Porch
8 Garage
9 Master bedroom
10 Bedroom
11 Study
12 Library
13 Master bathroom
14 Laundry
15 Gallery

Opposite top Second floor plan
Opposite bottom First floor plan
Top Entrance court
Above The house at night

A new kitchen and family room, set high above grade, look out to adjacent treetops. From within these spaces, one gets the impression of being in a tree house.

Privacy from the public was an important goal of the owners. Each space was carefully sited and screened to provide privacy while maintaining a close connection to outdoor living.

- Zone the house to separate private from public areas. Provide appropriate levels of visual and acoustic privacy.
- Use landscape in conjunction with architectural form to create exterior spaces.
- Plan and design the house being mindful of its appearance, not only during the day, but at night and in all seasons.

Left Winter view

Top Tree house view from family room dining area

Left Morning light in the forested glade

House in Remington Forest

This house in New Jersey sits in a grass covered glade in the heart of Remington forest. Part of a planned community, the design was subject to architectural guidelines and a stringent design review process intended to ensure compliance with regional building customs. Although the review process was sometimes tedious, it led to a helpful understanding of how to ensure harmony with the community's objectives.

- Be open to a wide range of ideas. Don't be critical too quickly, as seemingly inappropriate ideas often trigger useful and unanticipated possibilities.

The peaceful quality of the forest site and its natural landscape was an important consideration in the design. The house is carefully sited to fit into the landscape with a minimum of disturbance. Floors step down gently to accommodate the sloping grade.

- Be minimally disruptive to the landform.
- Preserve trees.

Stone, indigenous to the area, is used to help connect the house to the land. Deep recesses in the stone walls capture the breadth and solid nature of the stone material. Natural slate is used for the roof, which is designed with one-story eaves and dormer windows to reduce the scale of the house.

- Think about how daylight will affect the appearance of the form of the house. Use recesses, offsets, setbacks, projections and overhangs as well as the natural textures of materials to enable light, shade and shadows to enrich the form.

Based on the principals of Feng Shui, blessed by the owners' Feng Shui master, all living spaces are oriented to the south and each has through ventilation and a variety of views to the surrounding natural setting. Interestingly, many of the Feng Shui guidelines reinforced and supported my own heuristics.

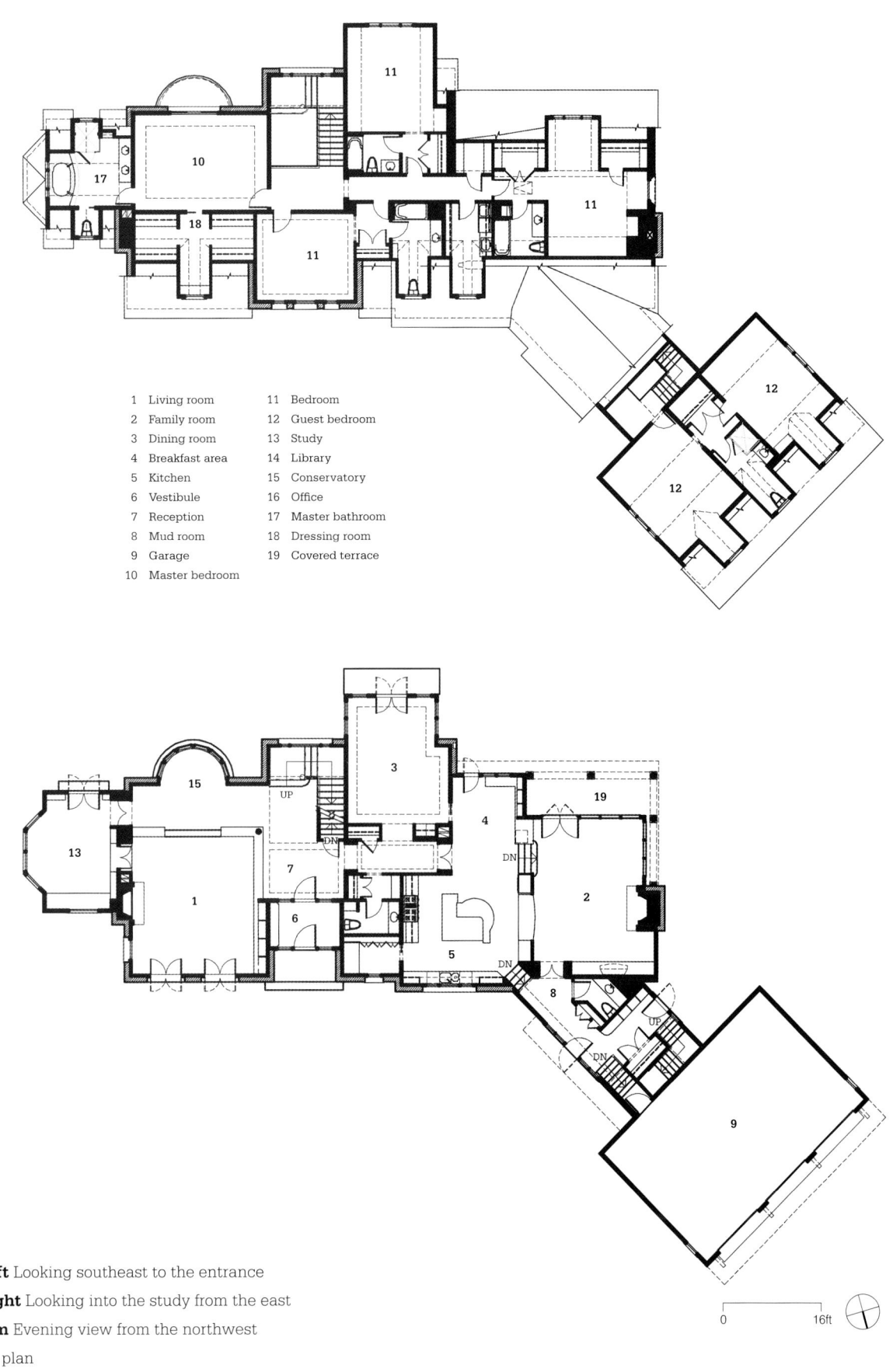

1 Living room
2 Family room
3 Dining room
4 Breakfast area
5 Kitchen
6 Vestibule
7 Reception
8 Mud room
9 Garage
10 Master bedroom
11 Bedroom
12 Guest bedroom
13 Study
14 Library
15 Conservatory
16 Office
17 Master bathroom
18 Dressing room
19 Covered terrace

Opposite top left Looking southeast to the entrance
Opposite top right Looking into the study from the east
Opposite bottom Evening view from the northwest
Top Second floor plan
Bottom First floor plan

House in Yarmouth

A half-acre site for a vacation home was selected by the owners for its proximity to Nantucket Sound and for its Cape Cod landscape of sea grass, reeds, pine trees and a small salt pond.

Utilizing an L-shaped plan, the house was designed to create an outside courtyard protected against strong prevailing southwesterly winds. A multipurpose storage wall forms one side of the courtyard and separates the court from service functions and vehicles.

- Site the house to take advantage of views and sunlight. Be cognizant of the direction of strong prevailing winds. Design outdoor living spaces protected from them.

Since access to the site was only by car, a heuristic that was important was that:

- The arrival experience should commence when one enters a property and not solely at the front door. The process of entering the site, being able to orient oneself and graciously arrive at a location that appropriately accommodates vehicles is the first step in a welcoming entrance sequence.

For this house, a vacation retreat, the intent was to totally isolate the vehicle area from the more tranquil environment within the house. The house was to be an oasis, divorcing itself from the customary activities of a busy life. Thus, one leaves one's car,

Right View of the house across the pond looking to Nantucket Sound

ascends some steps and passes through a barrier, physically and symbolically separating the inner courtyard and living areas of the house from the more frenzied outside world.

A sitting area shapes the core of this summer residence. In one direction, large glass doors open out to a bay and sandy beach, while to the other, a protected south-facing courtyard and pool are situated. Beyond the sitting area is the dining room with direct access to the courtyard for outdoor living.

A stair winds around the fireplace to the master bedroom area above. High windows with ventilating sash flood the space with light while allowing natural cross ventilation through the house. A large window above the fireplace brings light and distant water views to the upper level.

Left View of living area. Stair leads to master bedroom suite above

Above Guest bedroom with clerestory windows for light and ventilation

- Manipulate space and form to provide interest and delight. by balancing orderliness and visual clarity with the unexpected and unanticipated.
- In addition to maximizing views to the exterior, create vistas within the house.
- Think about where and how light, especially changing daylight, can articulate space and form. Consider the use of recesses, offsets, setbacks, projections and overhangs, as well as a variety of surface textures to create venues for light to enhance our perception of space and form. Contrast bright and reflective surfaces with darker more textured, shaded and shadowed ones. On the exterior, be aware of the path of the sun and how changing daylight will affect the design. On the interior, consider how to exploit the qualities of light to enrich the space and reinforce desired outcomes.

In this summer home, where hot weather is often uncomfortable, high ceilings are helpful, providing space for warm air to rise. Here, clerestory windows wash the high ceilings with light and allow a means for warm air to escape, enabling cooler air to be drawn in from below.

- In developing space and form, consider opportunities for secondary benefits (for example, utilizing the stack effect for natural ventilation).
- Design for cross ventilation and proper airflow.

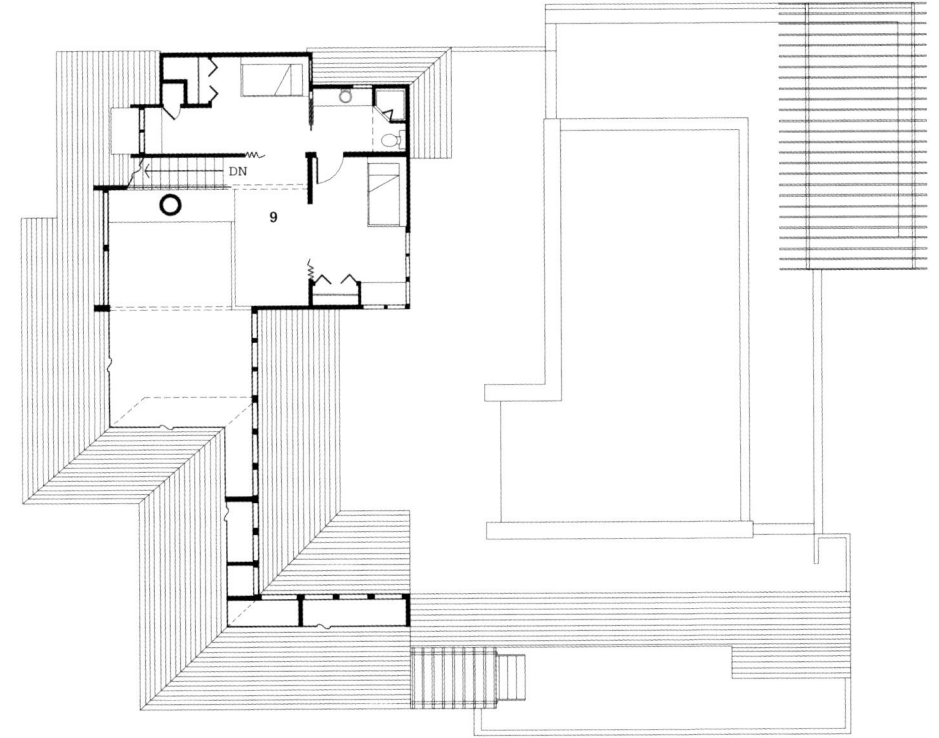

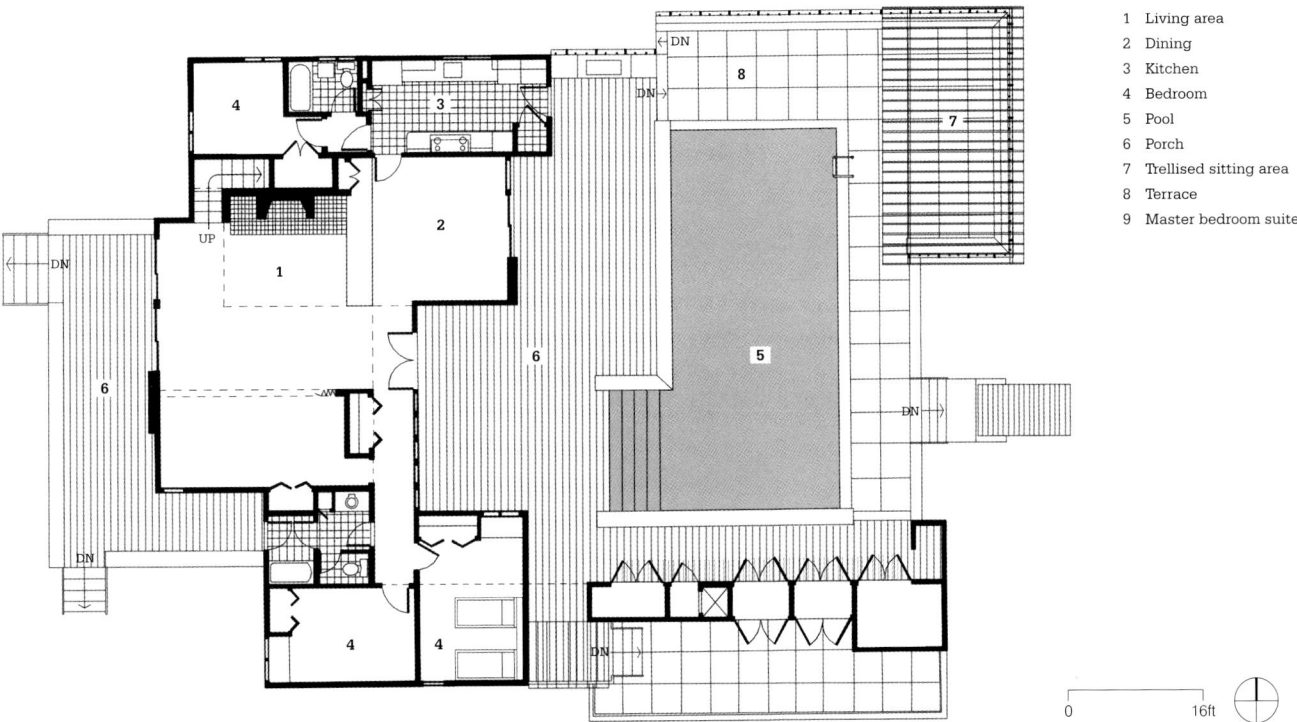

1 Living area
2 Dining
3 Kitchen
4 Bedroom
5 Pool
6 Porch
7 Trellised sitting area
8 Terrace
9 Master bedroom suite

Opposite Entry court and pool
Top Second floor plan
Bottom First floor plan

House on Beacon Hill

This historic carriage house was restored and converted to a new residence. Located in Boston's historic Beacon Hill district, no additional openings were permitted in the exterior facade. The result was a design that created a new, open interior courtyard with living spaces wrapped around it.

The ability to look out of the house was extremely limited, so visual relief was made possible by developing vistas within the house, especially into and through the courtyard. The resulting views were pleasing and unexpected as changing light conditions and circulation through and around the courtyard generated variety. This house reinforced, for me, the advantage of providing pleasing interior vistas within all my homes regardless of how extensive their exterior views might be.

- In addition to maximizing views to the exterior, design for vistas within the house.

Opposite New house built around a courtyard

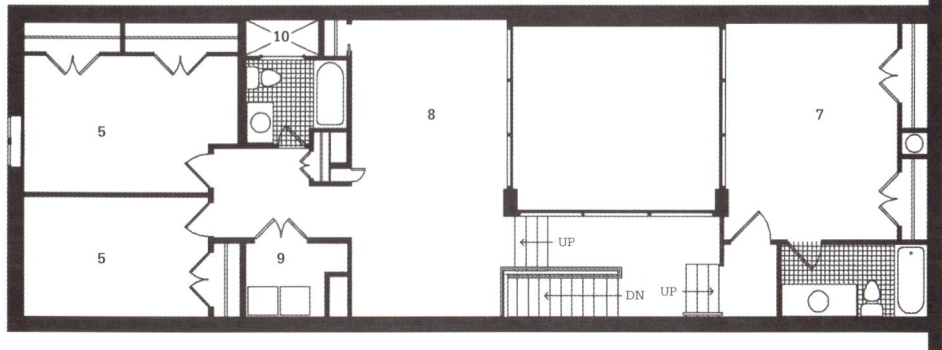
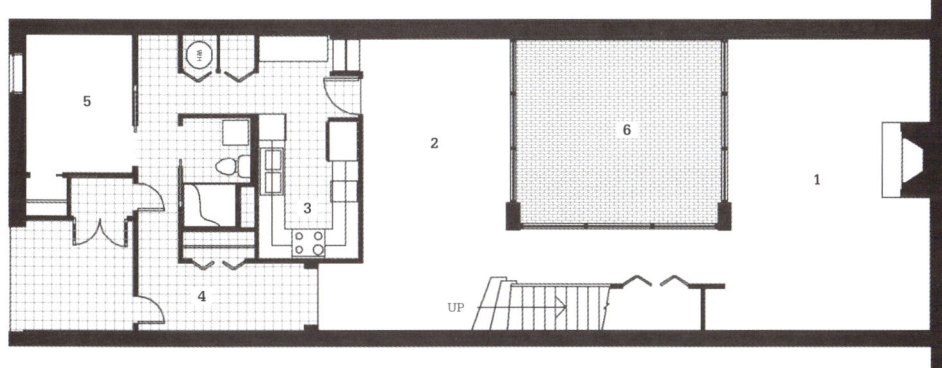

1. Living room
2. Dining
3. Kitchen
4. Entry foyer
5. Bedroom
6. Courtyard
7. Master bedroom
8. Sitting room / library
9. Laundry
10. Lightwell to below

Opposite Looking down into the courtyard with living spaces beyond

Top left View into the house and courtyard from the entry foyer

Top right Original historic façade integrated into the new design

Middle Second floor plan

Bottom First floor plan

House on Lake Erie

This house sits at the end of a long winding way overlooking Lake Erie. Here, everyone must arrive by car. A large, gracious entrance court welcomes guests and provides ample parking. Vehicles are separated and shielded from the house by landscaping and a low screen wall. A spacious and weather-protected entrance is easily identifiable. The owners' cars and garage are off to the side of the house, out of sight.

- Separate areas used for vehicular movement from ones used by pedestrians.

On the lakeside, the house opens out to the expansive view. A large, unbroken terrace, set slightly raised for better sightlines, provides all areas of the house with the opportunity to have direct access to the outdoors. Large stone chimneys and steep overhanging roofs give the house the sense of being a sheltered place. Although a grand house, carefully detailed elements and simple textured materials help create a gracious, human scale.

Left The house sits on raised ground over looking Lake Erie

Designing large homes is frequently more difficult than designing smaller ones. For larger homes, issues of scale need to be managed carefully to avoid unwanted monumentality. The larger massing often needs to be reduced into smaller, more residentially sized elements. These elements then need to be caringly reconnected and integrated. Too many pieces with weak transitions can result in disorder. Too few, and the house can become monumental and out of scale.

- Design to a human scale. Reduce perceived monumentality by articulating the overall mass into smaller more comprehensible components.
- Manipulate spaces and forms to provide interest and delight. Balance orderliness and visual clarity with the unexpected and unanticipated.

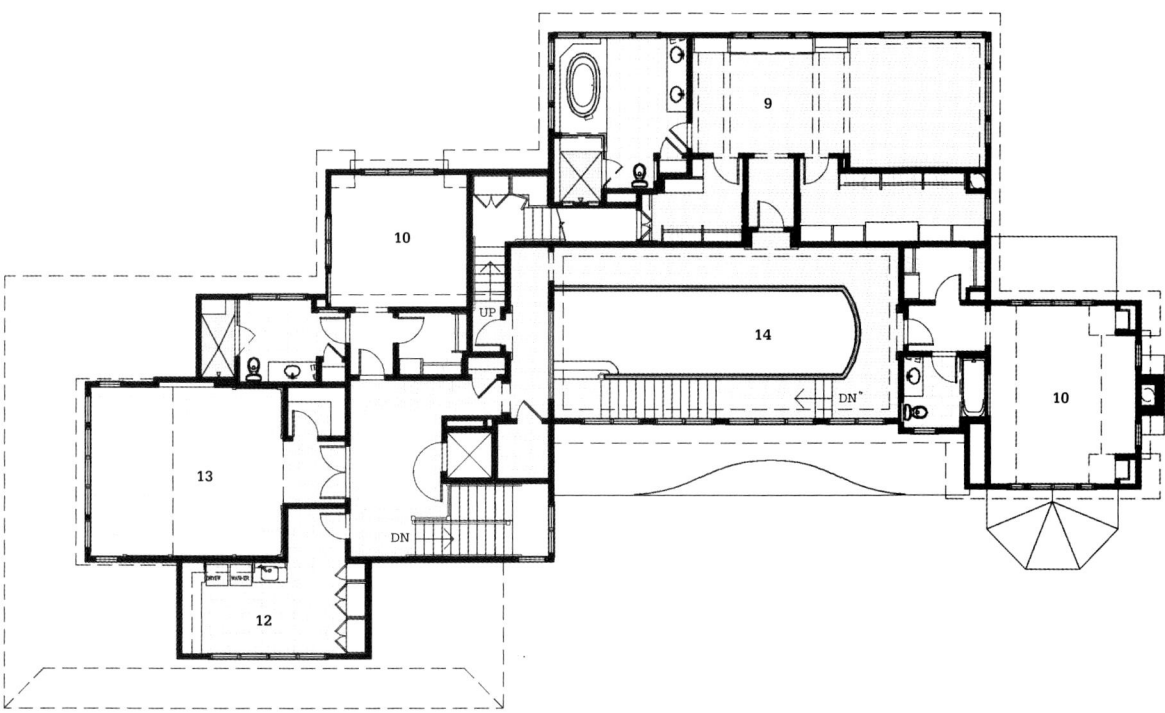

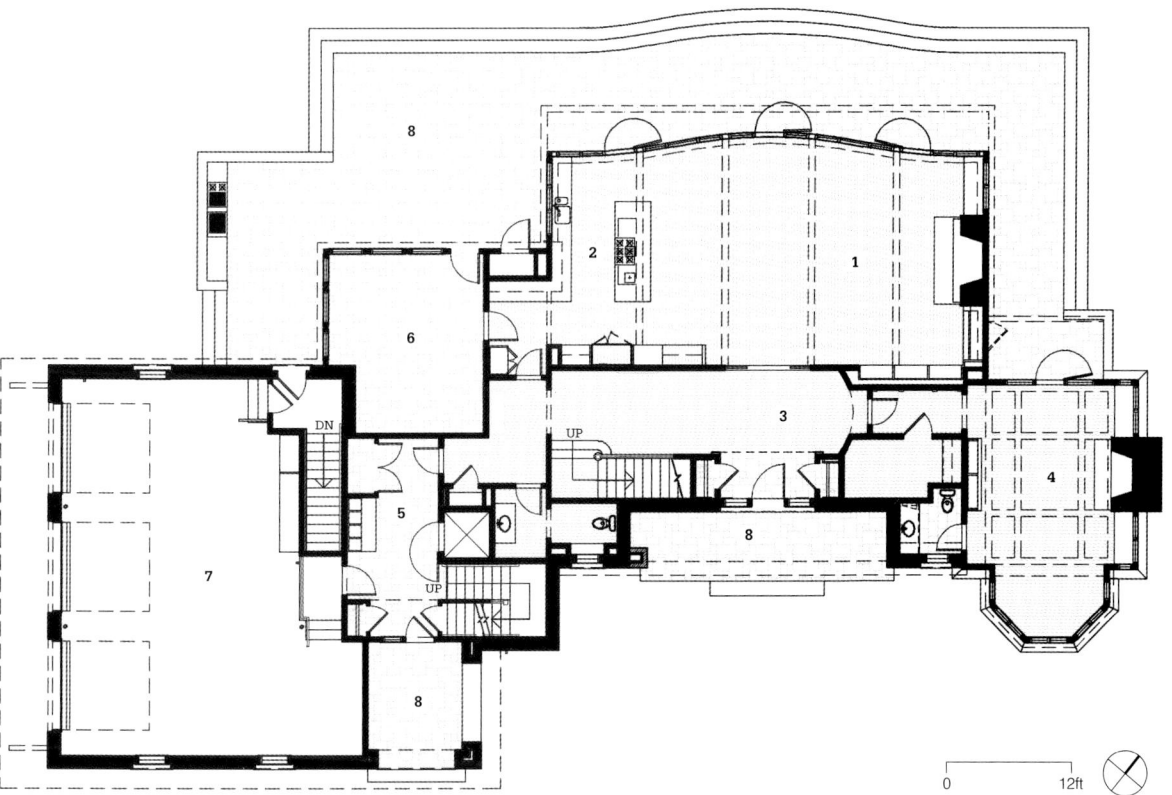

1 Greatroom
2 Kitchen
3 Gallery
4 Study
5 Mudroom
6 Screened porch
7 Garage
8 Terrace
9 Master bedroom suite
10 Bedroom
12 Laundry
13 Exercise
14 Open to below

Opposite top The entrance elevation with Lake Erie beyond
Opposite bottom A view of the house in the evening from the lake side
Top Second floor plan
Bottom First floor plan

House on Plum Island

- Design the house to take maximum advantage of views.

There was little choice where this house could be placed. Its site was a small lot, squeezed between two other homes, looking out to the Atlantic Ocean. There was some concern about privacy from next-door neighbors but the outstanding ocean views overcame any apprehension. The entire house was designed to maximize these exceptional views.

On the living floor, large glass doors and windows wrap around the corners of the house taking maximum advantage of the 180-degree scene. The floor of the kitchen (the rear portion of the living area space) is elevated to enable unobstructed views over the living area to the water beyond. Expansive glass and outdoor balconies on the upper floor further optimize the opportunities for enjoying the sea. At the top of the house, where vistas are above surrounding rooftops, a cupola retreat provides 360-degree panoramas with especially glorious western sunsets, a special getaway for family and friends.

- Be minimally disruptive to the landform.

For this house on a barrier island, so close to the water, respecting the existing landform was critical. The house is raised above the sand, elevated on piles, to enable wind to blow under and around the house forming protective sand dunes. These dunes help shelter the beach from erosion during tidal storms and are so critical that, for this house, the deck is shaped to defer to the contours of an adjacent dune.

Opposite Looking out to the Atlantic Ocean

Above Section view through the living area with kitchen floor lifted to afford better views to the ocean

Top Looking down on the deck, shaped to respect existing protective sand dune

Bottom left View from the cupola or lookout

Bottom right View to the ocean from the master bedroom

Opposite top Lookout floor plan

Opposite middle Second floor plan

Opposite bottom First floor plan

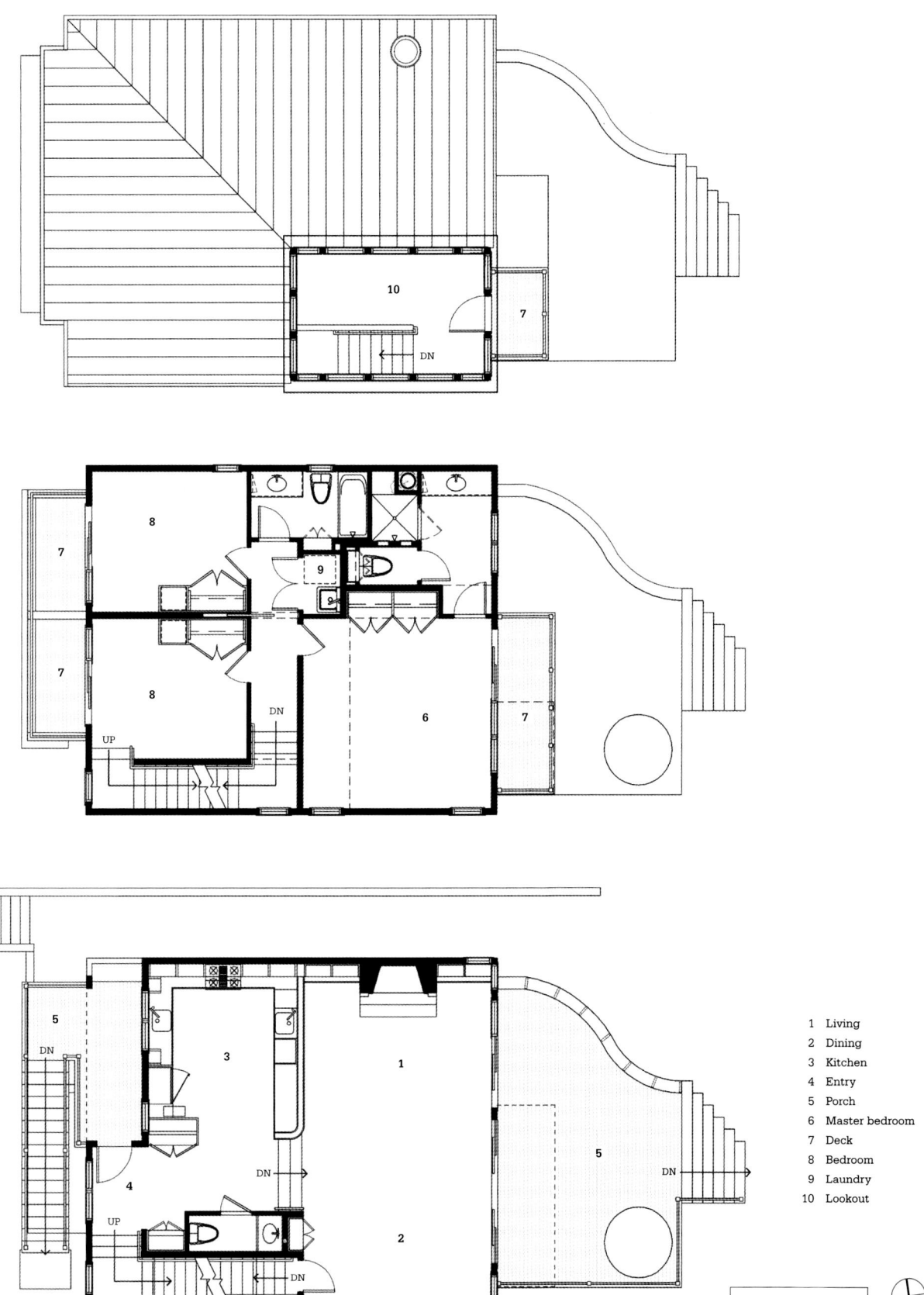

House on the Island of Vieques

Located on a mountainside in the Caribbean, this 3500-square-foot, two-level house is approached from above through a cluster of large volcanic boulders. These large rocks were so exceptional that they became part of the entrance sequence for the house. They influenced how the house was to be sited.

- Take advantage of unusual or special site features that may influence the design or even suggest a design direction.

The house is constructed from poured-in-place concrete and is finished with stucco, red tile flooring and mahogany trim, creating a distinct contrast to the surrounding lush vegetation. The design takes advantage of the warm climate for heat with natural ocean breezes providing ventilation and cooling.

A large flat roof affords protective shade from the strong sun and shelter for desired expanses of glass and outdoor living. The roof, specially insulated to keep the interiors cool, acts as a water collector for cisterns built into the foundations, which supply water for drinking, as well as household use and a swimming pool.

Right The wide flat roof designed to collect rainwater

An expansive roof was the resolution for these desired functional requirements. Beyond these necessities, the final form and appropriate expression of the roof required consideration of additional concerns. Some of these included: (1) arranging the house to fit the land and relate to the changing positions of the sun, (2) positioning walls to satisfy the prerequisites of anticipated activities, and (3) adjusting horizontal and vertical dimensions with careful thought for their proportions and the proper scale for the house.

The result is a functional and pleasurable composition with attractive proportions and interesting patterns of light and shade. The house fits comfortably into the landscape and projects a strong visual image feeling almost as if it is an extension of the earth.

- Let form evolve and be recognized as an expression of the functions being accommodated. Form does follow function, but needs to be fine-tuned and managed to ensure all issues, including aesthetics, are appropriately resolved. Let the aesthetic quality of the house grow out of an accommodation and integration of its functional needs, not by arbitrary applications of decorative shapes or appliqués.

Above The house with its wide protective roof looks out over the countryside

Opposite top The house sets down into the mountainside with minimal disruption to existing natural grades

Opposite bottom The entry to the house designed to exploit the exceptional uniqueness of large volcanic boulders

171

Thanks and Acknowledgements

I'd like to thank the many people who have assisted me in bringing this book to fruition. When writing a book, it's especially helpful to have a supportive and experienced family. My wife, Sandy, time and again, thoughtfully reviewed my many drafts with her critical eye, continually adding her encouragement. She also provided a unique capacity to unearth just the right poetic quotation to reinforce the ideas I was trying to highlight. Special thanks also to my sons Jonathan and David for taking the time to forage through my early texts and provide pragmatic advice for making my writing more down-to-earth and understandable, and to my daughter Louisa who assisted me with her artistic talents, in particular her illustration and graphics expertise. Of course, having three younger generation, computer-techy children who can solve frustrating computer glitches is also very helpful. I have learned so much from them.

Others also lent great support. Thanks and gratitude to my friend, Ann McLaughlin, for steering me in the right direction. Her early reviews guided me to make text and drawings more comprehensible and readable. I strongly recommend that anyone thinking of writing a book make friends with a wise librarian. My sincere appreciation to Susan Diesenhouse for her expert editing of the final text. It continues to amaze me that there are people who have the ability to find just the right selection and arrangement of words to express an idea. Thanks also to Andy Chipman. Without his help in the graphic organization and layout of the book, it would never have been so well done. And thank you Emily Cotter for your thoughtful help providing all those things I needed to get done but didn't even know I needed.

I also would like to recognize and thank the staff at CBT, whose architectural expertise and efforts helped bring these houses to realization. I apologize if I have left anyone out due to missing records. Special thanks to Ellen Perko for overseeing so many of these houses. Thanks also to Maury Childs, Charles Tseckares, Jim McBain, Alfred Wojciechowski, Frank Coyne, Chris Coios, Mark Donegan, David Hancock, Lois Goodell, Ryan Duell, Kristen Foley, Mark Hellen, Betsy Redman, Catherine Hunt, Matt Jackson, Maria Mak, David Rubenstein, Adi Toledano, Aaron Williams, Joan Valle, Rick Greenlee, Erin Kennedy, Scott Thompson, Sam Batchelor, Neal Krause, Jamie Pennington, Kevin Wu, Robert Lang, Elizabeth Mortenson, Haim Izraeli, Eric Jahan, Howard Kozloff, Stanley Kubinski, Elizabeth Loeb, Kevin Lynch, Eric Rasmussen, Matthew Tharp, Jesse Yan, Tony Barletta, June Komisar, Darrin Ohanesian, Guy Sturgis, Tim Washburn, Paul Weber, Kathryn Friedman, David Nagahiro, Chris Hill, Pa Kou Lee, Jackie McGee, Blair Caple, John Altieri, Elizabeth Bradley, Patrick Banks, Rob Bramhall, Greg Albertson, Dennis Allain, Kent Duckham, Byron Kim, William Mullany, Clay Smook, Craig Sweeny, Jonathan Knickerbocker, Liam O'Sullivan, Ron Barkey, Selena Goldberg, Alice Harris, Ron Payne, David Madson, Eric Vogel, Haril Pandya, Kishore Varanasi, Margaret Deutsch, Paul Viccica, Phil Casey and David Ferris. Working with all of you was a pleasure for me.

Photography Credits

Finally, I would like to give credit to the talented photographers who so beautifully photographed the houses shown in this book:

Implementing the Design: Richard Mandelkorn, Aerial: Mark Flannery

House in Woods Hole: Edward Jacoby, Aerial: Mark Flannery

House in Weston: Edward Jacoby

House in Dartmouth: Richard Mandelkorn, Aerial: Mark Flannery

House in Mattapoisett: Nick Wheeler, Richard Mandelkorn, Aerial: Randolf Foulds

House on Martha's Vineyard: Edward Jacoby

House in the Berkshire Mountains: Edward Jacoby, Aerial: Mark Flannery

House in Chestnut Hill: Richard Mandelkorn

House in Remington Forest: Edward Jacoby

House in Yarmouth: George Zimberg

House on Beacon Hill: Richard Mandelkorn

House on Lake Erie: Kevin Reeves

House on Plum Island: Trent Bell

House on the Island of Vieques: Maury Childs

Every effort has been made to trace the original source of copyright material contained in this book. The publishers would be pleased to hear from copyright holders to rectify any errors or omissions.

The information and illustrations in this publication have been prepared and supplied by the author. While all reasonable efforts have been made to source the required information and ensure accuracy, the publishers do not, under any circumstances, accept responsibility for errors, omissions, and representations, express or implied.